1

THE ECONOMICS OF LAND TENURE IN GEORGIA

STUDIES IN HISTORY, ECONOMICS AND PUBLIC LAW

EDITED BY THE FACULTY OF POLITICAL SCIENCE OF
COLUMBIA UNIVERSITY

Volume XXIII] [Number 1

THE
ECONOMICS OF LAND TENURE
IN GEORGIA

BY

ENOCH MARVIN BANKS

AMS PRESS
NEW YORK

COLUMBIA UNIVERSITY
STUDIES IN THE
SOCIAL SCIENCES

58

The Series was formerly known as *Studies in History, Economics and Public Law.*

Reprinted with the permission of Columbia University Press
From the edition of 1905, New York
First AMS EDITION published 1968
Manufactured in the United States of America

Library of Congress Catalogue Card Number: 68-56647

AMS PRESS, INC.
New York, N.Y. 10003

PREFACE

THE following investigation has been confined to a relatively small territory in order to give greater precision and definiteness to the discussion. There are other states in which the land tenure arrangements are similar to those in Georgia. The conclusions reached in respect to this particular state may be applied, therefore, with modifications more or less slight, to the other states similarly circumstanced.

As this study was assuming its final form valuable criticisms and suggestions were made by Professors Edwin R. A. Seligman, John B. Clark, Henry R. Seager, Henry L. Moore and Dr. Alvin S. Johnson, to each of whom the author acknowledges his indebtedness. Acknowledgement is also hereby made of assistance received from the Carnegie Institution of Washington in the collection of materials for this monograph. Thanks are due the Comptroller-General of Georgia, Mr. Wm. A. Wright, for the courtesies extended in granting access to the tax archives of the state. The author is also indebted to his nephew, Mr. William N. Banks, of Grantville, Georgia, for services rendered at various stages of the work. Friends in Georgia, too numerous to mention by name, have given valuable assistance in answering the many inquiries addressed to them. The author hereby expresses his appreciation of their help.

E. M. B.

COLUMBIA UNIVERSITY, *March*, 1905.

CONTENTS

CHAPTER I

PAGE

THE TENURE OF LAND BEFORE 1860

CHAPTER II

TENDENCIES IN THE OWNERSHIP OF LAND AMONG THE WHITES SINCE THE WAR

CHAPTER III

THE INFLUENCE OF THE CREDIT SYSTEM ON LANDOWNERSHIP

CHAPTER IV

THE GENESIS AND DEVELOPMENT OF LANDOWNERSHIP AMONG THE NEGROES

CHAPTER V

THE SYSTEMS OF FARMING BASED ON THE RELATION OF THE FARMER TO THE SOIL

PAGE

CHAPTER VI

THE ECONOMIC WORKINGS OF THE SYSTEMS OF LAND TENURE

CHAPTER I

THE TENURE OF LAND BEFORE 1860

GEORGIA as a colony developed and transmitted to Georgia as a state two institutions of great importance in their bearings upon the problem of land tenure. These were unrestricted landownership and negro slavery.

A humanitarian motive led to the founding of the colony. Back of the motive and giving rise to it was an economic condition. The colony as planned by its promoters was for the relief and rehabilitation of an unfortunate debtor class. A fresh opportunity in the midst of a new environment was to be given those who had failed in the economic life struggle in England. In view of the special purposes for which the colony was planted, it was thought proper by those in authority to make certain regulations respecting the tenure of land. It was desired to establish upon this territory not a landed aristocracy, but a self-supporting land-owning citizenry. To this end the charter itself placed a maximum limitation upon the number of acres that could be granted to one person. It stipulated "that no greater quantity of lands be granted, either entirely or in parcels, to or for the use, or in trust for any one person, than five hundred acres."[1]

The charter regulations touching land grants were, however, of a general character—the details were very

[1] *Georgia Historical Collections*, vol. ii, p. 190; Jones, *History of Georgia*, vol. i, p. 108; Stevens, *History of Ga.*, vol. i, p. 64.

properly left to be determined by the trustees of the colony. Upon military and economic grounds they decided to grant land in lots of fifty acres each.[1] Furthermore, provision was made

> to prevent the accumulation of several lots into one hand lest the garrison should be lessened, and likewise to prevent a division of those lots into smaller parcels lest that which was no more than sufficient for one planter, when entire, should if divided amongst several, be too scanty for their subsistence.

To effect these ends estates were granted "in tail male." The charter said that no person should be granted over five hundred acres of land; while the incorporators in making use of the principle involved in this chartered limitation said that one person could possess only fifty acres, and that he could not dispose of his holding in any ordinary manner.

It was also stipulated that no person holding land in Georgia could "hire, keep, lodge, board, or employ within the limits of the colony any negroes whether slave or otherwise except with the special leave of the common council."[3] It was expected that those to whom grants were made would come over to claim and cultivate personally the lands given.[4]

The colony did not flourish. It was soon discovered that the restrictions created a condition unfavorable to the economic prosperity of the settlers. Only five years after the founding of the colony a memorial signed by many of the settlers making complaint of the discourag-

[1] "An Account Showing the Progress of the Colony" (1741). Reprinted in *Ga. Hist. Col.*, vol. ii, pp. 275, 276.

[2] *Ibid.*, p. 276.

[3] Jones, *Hist. of Ga.*, vol. i, p. 159.

[4] *Ibid.*, p. 107.

ing situation of things was sent to the trustees.[1] Instead of a peasantry growing stronger and more self-sustaining, indebtedness was developing together with a desire to pledge lands as security for further advances. As a means of escape from the evil state of things into which they had come, the petitioners asked for two privileges: (1) To hold lands in fee simple; (2) to introduce negro slavery.[2] According to their arguments the first would enable them to obtain credit, while the second would place them in command of cheap labor, and thus make it possible for them to compete in industry with their neighbors of South Carolina. The trustees displayed greater willingness to give heed to the representations from the colony concerning land tenure than to those touching the need of slaves. In view of the urgency of the situation, they took steps at once to modify the rigidness of the law relating to the tenure of land.[3] Other modifications were made soon thereafter, so that by 1750 the principle of absolute ownership of land was recognized in the colony.[4]

The year before this in answer to an appeal made by some of the inhabitants of Georgia and because of the unprogressive, or more properly the retrogressive, condition of the colony, the trustees gave their consent for the settlers to hold and use slaves under certain regulations guaranteeing their humane treatment, and under other provisions looking to the welfare and safety of the

[1] "A True and Historical Narrative of the Colony of Ga." (1741). Reprinted in *Ga. Hist. Col.*, vol. ii, p. 217 *et seq.*

[2] *Ibid.*, p. 220.

[3] *Ga. Hist. Collections*, vol. ii, pp. 300, 234.

[4] Jones, *Hist. of Ga.*, vol. i, p. 422, and Stevens, *Hist. of Ga.*, vol. i, p. 281.

colony when this new and barbarous element should become a part of its population.

It is said that the effect of the above-mentioned changes was instantaneous. The current of migration was reversed. Instead of leaving the colony in large numbers to seek better conditions elsewhere as they had been doing, settlers, upon learning of the changes, turned to Georgia. So effective were the stimuli that within three years after the new order of things had been established the reports indicate a doubling of the population;[1] within ten years there had been a fivefold increase,[2] and by 1766 it was estimated that there were 10,000 whites and 8,000 negroes in the colony as compared with a total population of about 2,000 in 1750.[3]

Such in brief outline was the course of development through which the unrestricted private ownership of land was effected, and through which the institution of negro slavery was established in Georgia. The first is still regarded, whether justly or not, by a majority of civilized mankind as a prerequisite to the highest human welfare. The second has served its purpose, and has been discarded as an unjustifiable economic institution. Since this essay centers in some of the problems involved in the first of these two institutions, and inasmuch as the establishment and subsequent overthrow of the second has added so many complications and peculiar phases to these problems, their early beginnings are of more than passing interest.

After the severance from England and even while the

[1] Evidence quoted in Stevens, *Hist. of Ga.*, vol. i, p. 313, and in Jones, *Hist of Ga.*, vol. i, p. 460.

[2] Jones, *Hist. of Ga.*, vol. i, p. 541.

[3] Stevens, *Hist. of Ga.*, vol. ii, p. 53.

revolutionary contest was in progress, the state government adopted a policy the purpose of which was to encourage a further increase of a stable population. This was the so-called head-right system of grants. The preamble to an act opening a land office, passed in 1777, says:

Whereas there remains much vacant and uncultivated land in this state, the settlement of which is of the highest importance, wherefore it becomes necessary that all due encouragement should be given to persons who come and settle in this state, and by that means promote the increase of its inhabitants.[1]

According to this act every head of a family was allowed to select and to come into possession of two hundred acres of unoccupied land and fifty additional acres for each member of his family, provided he would pay the expenses of surveying the plot, and provided, also, he would occupy with his family the land thus taken. Other acts of the same general tenor were passed from time to time in the latter part of the eighteenth century.[2]

The section of the state settled under the operation of these laws lies south of Hall and Habersham counties and east of the Oconee and Ocmulgee rivers, the latter forming the western boundary only after the Oconee flows into it. This part of the state was, therefore, first settled; here the lands have been longest under fee simple ownership. In this region are to be found thus early the beginnings of the large estates of a later period, for even slaves up to the number of ten were reckoned members of the family in the allotment of fifty additional acres for each member. The terms of occu-

[1] Prince, *Digest of the Laws of Ga.* (1837), pp. 517-519.

[2] *Ibid.*, pp. 519-540.

pancy and possession were easy, for, owing to the abundance of the land and the scanty population, it was the purpose of the acts to induce settlers to come.

The other part of the state was parceled, and came into the possession of individuals under the operation of land lottery acts. In order to encourage the peopling of the western part of the state a liberal system of land distribution was practiced as fast as the Indian claims were extinguished. In all there were eight distributions of land made at intervals from 1803 to 1833.[1] The general plan, according to which these allotments were made, is not only interesting as a bit of history, but has an essential bearing upon the central theme of this essay. The spirit of the plan may be seen from the provisions of the first land lottery act, that, namely, of May, 1803, providing for the disposition of the lands acquired the preceding year from the Creek Indians.[2] The lands consisted of two separate strips, one in the central part of the state and the other in the southeastern corner. The first tract, including parts of what are now Morgan, Putnam, Baldwin, Wilkinson and Laurens counties, was to be surveyed and divided into ten land districts, and these into square lots of two hundred and two and one-half acres each. Likewise a second tract was to be laid off into three land districts, and these into lots containing four hundred and ninety acres each. Since there were not enough plots to grant one to each person, and since it was considered desirable to give each man equal chances of sharing in the state's bounty, and since the lottery idea was characteristic of the times, it is not surprising to find that the act pro-

[1] Lottery Acts may be found in Prince, *Digest of Ga. Laws* (1837), pp. 545-568.

[2] Prince, *Digest of Ga. Laws* (1822), p. 284.

vided for the distribution of the land through the drawing of lots. The lot numbers were to be placed in "the wheels" together with a sufficient number of blanks to give every person so entitled one or two draws.

The act recited that every free white male person twenty-one years old or over, if a citizen of the United States, and an inhabitant of Georgia for at least one year preceding the act, should be allowed one draw. In case such a person had a family he might have two draws. Likewise widows with children might have two draws; families of orphans, one draw; revolutionary officers and soldiers, two draws. The fees required of successful drawers before they could come into full ownership of the land were small. By paying into the treasury the sum of four dollars per one hundred acres "in lieu of all fees of office and other charges for surveying and granting said lands," the prize drawers received titles to their respective tracts.

As indicated above, the general tenor of the other lottery acts was similar to the first. Later eighteen instead of twenty-one was made the minimum drawing age, and three years' residence in the state instead of one was required of the drawers. A most important provision of subsequent acts was that those who had drawn lots in previous distributions were not to be allowed further drawing privileges. Each lottery act named a period within which the grants had to be taken out. Failure to take out the grants within the period specified would result in reversion of the lands to the state. Notwithstanding the last-mentioned provision of each act an authoritative writer in 1837 said that "the privilege of taking out grants has been continued by annual revivals down to the present time."

[1] Prince, *Digest of Ga. Laws* (1837), p. 568.

A rough estimate seems to indicate that about 130,000 lots were made available through these lottery acts. In order to make the estimate a little more detailed, the following figures are given:

Lottery acts. Year	Size of lots in acres	Estimated number of lots made available, by size	Estimated number of acres distributed
1803	202½	4,000	810,000
	490	1,100	539,000
1806	202½	9,300	209,250
1818	250	17,500	4,375,000
	490	10,000	4,900,000
1819	250	1,100	275,000
	490	500	245,000
1821	202½	12,200	2,470,500
1825	202½	21,000	4,252,500
1830	160	18,300	2,928,000
1831	40	35,000	1,400,000
Total	172.3	130,000	22,404,250

If 130,000 landless persons had each entered into the possession and utilization of a lot of land under this system of distribution, the result of such an experiment would have been most interesting. The actual result is only slightly less interesting when allowance is made for certain qualifying circumstances arising from the conditions under which the distribution was made. First, some who drew lots already owned land; secondly, some who drew lots never came into possession of them; thirdly, some drew as many as two lots. These qualifying circumstances are given in the order of their importance. Those who held lands under the head-right grants or who had bought lands were not excluded from participating in the chances of getting more in the lotteries. Many whose lands had become more or less exhausted because of exploitative methods of cultivation, were inspired through a fortunate draw to move to fresher and stronger soils.[1] Many who drew prizes failed to take out their grants. As indicated above it was provided that fortunate drawers must take out their grants within a certain period, else they would revert to the state. Many acts supplementary to the general lottery acts were passed for the purpose of extending these time limitations, and many other acts were passed for the purpose of reducing the fees connected with the taking out of grants.[2] All of which goes to show conclusively that there was not a universal eagerness among the successful drawers to take possession of their lands. In many instances the claims lapsed, and the lands reverted to the state and were subsequently sold to others.[3] In other cases the grants were completed, but the grantees disposed of the lands thus obtained without even seeing them. In still other cases the lands drawn in the lottery were so poor or so badly situated, that it was thought useless to have the titles made out. Some of the cases of reversion, however, can be explained only on grounds of improvidence. The fee of a few dollars incident to taking out the grants and the energy required in establishing themselves upon a new territory, were in such cases too great a tax upon the easy-going spirits.

The close of Georgia's policy of land distribution

[1] It would take a very detailed investigation into the most hidden sources of information to get any trustworthy data on which to base an estimate of just what percentage of those who drew lots were already owners of land.

[2] Prince, *Digest of Ga. Laws* (1837), pp. 545-568.

[3] The records in the office of the secretary of state show this. The gentleman now in charge of these records suggested to the writer that perhaps twenty-five per cent of the lands reverted in this manner to the state.

found a situation far from ideal. There were not 130,000 landholders owning, occupying and cultivating 130,000 lots of land averaging in size one hundred and seventy-five acres. Instead the situation was about as follows, in part good and in part bad:

1. A very considerable body of newly-created landowners.

2. The continued existence of many landless persons.

3. The increased holdings of many who already held land.

4. Reverted lands at the disposal of the state.

5. A condition favorable to the further enlargement of the holdings of those skilful in the management of their affairs.

It is impossible to obtain figures that would indicate even approximately the extent to which land tended to be massed in large holdings before the war.[1] The United States census for 1860 attempted to give figures bearing on the number and size of farms in the state, and this is the best available source of information on the subject. These returns, classified according to the acreage of improved land, in the farms, are as follows:[2]

Total number of farms	53,897
3 and under 10 acres	906
10 to 20	2,803
20 to 50	13,644
50 to 100	14,129
100 to 500	18,821
500 to 1000	2,692
1000 acres and over	902

[1] The county tax digests kept at the state capitol did not come safely through the war. The information might be abstracted from them if they were available.

[2] *Eighth Census* (1860), *Agriculture*, p. 196.

According to the census the total farm acreage of the state was 26,650,490, about one-third of which, 8,062,758 acres, was classed as improved land. As indicated above, the foregoing classification had reference only to the improved land in farms. In order to make the figures applicable to entire holdings, including the unimproved as well as the improved acreage, the figures would have to undergo a considerable shifting downward. It is likely that a five-fold increase of the farms containing over one thousand acres would bring the number of these large holdings within a reasonable range of accuracy. Likewise the number in the five hundred to one thousand-acre group should be multiplied by three in order to make it indicate the probable number of holdings within the group.

Inasmuch as the total number of farms may be assumed to represent, roughly at least, the total number of landowners, the changes just mentioned will necessitate a readjustment of the numbers of the smaller groups. Such an assumption, however, gives only an approximation to the number of landowners; because, in the first place, some lands were held speculatively, and hence were not reckoned as farms, and, secondly, in some cases, two or more farms may have been operated on one holding through some plan of tenancy. Thus while the average number of utilized acres in the farms was only about one hundred and fifty, the census figures indicate that the average size of holdings was four hundred and thirty acres.[1]

As to geographical distribution, it may be said that in practically all the counties south and east of a line extending from Hart county to Chattahoochee county the

[1] *Eighth Census, Agriculture*, p. 222.

average size of holdings was above four hundred and thirty acres, whereas in all the counties, except four, to the north and west of this line the average was below four hundred and thirty acres. The larger holdings were, therefore, to be found in the region of the head-right grants and in that section where the lottery grants were largest, that is to say, practically all the territory where the plots granted contained four hundred and ninety and two hundred and fifty acres, and in some of the territory where they contained two hundred and two and one-half acres.

If a map of Georgia constructed to show the average size of holdings by counties in 1860, is compared with a map showing the size of plots granted under the several lottery acts, it is found that in most of the counties the holdings on the average were then at least twice as large as the original grants. Upon the whole the one hundred and sixty-acre plots had hardly doubled in size. This was largely due to the fact that they lay in the uninviting mountainous counties of the north. The forty-acre grants, just south of the one hundred and sixty-acre lots, had undergone on the average a merging of from four to eight into one holding. So also the two hundred and two and one-half, the two hundred and fifty, and even the four hundred and ninety-acre lots are shown to have had a considerable tendency towards merging. While four hundred and thirty acres represents a very large average holding, it should be remembered that only about one-fourth or one-fifth of the owners held tracts of land larger than this average—the vast majority of holdings ranged below it.

The *Eighth Census* gives some figures on the ownership of slaves in Georgia, which make an interesting revelation when compared with the figures given above on the number and grouping of farms. A résumé of these figures shows that there were 41,084 slave-owners holding 462,198 slaves—an average of 11.2 slaves to each owner. A grouping of these owners according to the number of slaves held by each is here presented:[1]

Number of slave-owners	Number of slaves owned by each	Number of slave-owners	Number of slaves owned by each
6,713	1	2,823	15 to 20
4,355	2	2,910	20 to 30
3,482	3	1,400	30 to 40
2,984	4	739	40 to 50
2,543	5	729	50 to 70
2,213	6	373	70 to 100
1,839	7	181	100 to 200
1,647	8	23	200 to 300
1,415	9	7	300 to 500
4,707	10 to 15	1	over 500

A distribution of the slave groups among the farm groups upon the basis of making each farm, beginning with the largest, represent a slave-owner, so long as the latter last, gives the following result:

	Number of farms	*Number of slaves per farm*
3 to 10 acres	906	
10 to 20 acres	2,803	
20 to 50 acres	13,644	1[2]
50 to 100 acres	14,129	2 to 6
100 to 500 acres	18,821	6 to 30
500 to 1000 acres	2,692	30 to 60
1000 acres and over	901	60 to 500

[1] *Eighth Census* (1860), *Agriculture*, p. 227.

[2] In many cases the owner of only one slave was not a farmer. Even aside from this the number of owners of one slave is not large enough to correspond to the number of farms in the 20 to 50 acre group.

It thus appears that while the total number of active farms was 53,887, the total number of slave-owners was 41,084. Now, since many of the slave-holders with only a slave or two resided in towns and held no farms, it is evident that there must have been in the neighborhood of 15,000 farmers working without the aid of slave labor. It is possible that a few of these were tenants, but it is more than probable that an overwhelming majority of them were relatively small landowners cultivating their own acres.

If a map of the state is drawn and the counties shaded in which the average number of slaves held per slave-holder is over the average for the state, and then another map is drawn with counties shaded in which the number of farms exceeds the number of slaveholders by one hundred, it is found that the shading overlaps in only a few cases. This shows that the region in which farms worked by their proprietors tended to prevail more than elsewhere was outside the region characterized by large possessions of lands and slaves. Moreover, such farms prevailed in the rugged region of the north and the pine flats of the south, each of which was relatively uninviting from the economic point of view. On the other hand, the region of much land and many slaves embraced the seaboard counties and a belt of counties running through the middle of the state in a southwesterly direction, together with several counties in the southwestern corner of the state. It was, therefore, in the cotton and rice sections that the slavery plantation system predominated. Even here, however, it must be remembered, the small farm existed side by side with the large plantation.

There was no sharp line of demarcation between the planters and the farmers of Georgia. As a general thing, it may be said that the planter's acres could be counted by the thousands and his slaves by the scores. Such a characterization makes the number of real planters very small when compared with the total number of farmers in the state. In every county there were gradations in the area of holdings from a few acres up to thousands of acres. In every county there were gradations in the number of slaves held, from one up to fifteen, and in most counties there were from one up to fifty slaves per slaveholder. These gradations obscured any exact lines of stratification. The door of opportunity was always open for the man of push and purpose.[1]

Less than the lifetime of a generation elapsed between the last land lottery and the revolution of the sixties. During this period, as has been indicated above, large holdings continued to be built up in number and size, owing to the relative abundance of land and the economies of supervised large-scale production.

All absolute standards both of morality and economy condemn slavery. Regarded relatively, however, that is to say, in relation to certain times and circumstances the institution may be both beneficent and efficient. Without doubt slavery in the South was rapidly becoming an anachronism. But in the crusade against the institution the economist came to the aid of the moralist, and in an exaggerated manner presented against the system two main arguments—mutually contradictory in their bearings upon the the economics of the problem. One had reference to the inability of non-slaveholders to compete with slaveholders; the other had reference to the unprofitableness of slave labor. The first point contains an

[1] For a view of the situation somewhat similar to that here given see U. B. Phillips, *Georgia and State Rights*, p. 107.

essential truth pertinent to conditions in Georgia as well as to the growth of large plantations. In order to state correctly the basis of the advantage the matter must be subjected to a little closer analysis than has usually been made.

The small proprietor of land was at a disadvantage in competing with the planter, but not primarily because the planter was in command of "cheaper labor." Of course, whenever and wherever profits exist there is usually "cheap labor," but it is the tendency of competition to eliminate such profits by ultimately imputing them to labor and capital. It is a mistake to suppose that in the case of the planter the labor cost of production was expressed merely in the food, shelter and clothing of the slave. At the end of each year a specific part of the product of the industry was imputable to the labor of the slave. The value of the slave was determined upon the basis of this imputed product after deducting the expenses connected with the maintenance of the slave as well as a sinking fund against his wear and tear. Interest on this capitalized value of the slave was, therefore, as important an element in the cost of production as was the food, shelter and clothing of the slave. In those cases where the product was unusually large, thus giving rise to considerable profits, competition operated to cause entrepreneurs, in order to participate in such profits, to increase the number of their slaves. In this way profits were cut down, and there tended to be a normal product per unit of slave labor. It thus appears that the entire net product imputable to the labor of the slave really tended to be an element of expense in production. This product was large, and consequently the labor cost per unit of product was comparatively small, on account of the form of organization. It was, therefore, the system of supervised large-scale production rather than slavery *per se* that gave the planter an advantage over the small proprietor. The labor expense involved in the production of a pound of cotton tended to be the same under slavery as would have been the case had competitive wages been paid under a system of plantation cultivation.

It may be added that the slavery-plantation system did not tend to have monopolistic powers, for the plantations remained competitive units with no attempt to lower the price of cotton in order to oust the small producer. But, notwithstanding this, the fact remains that the small farmer was at a disadvantage as compared with the planter, just as to-day, even aside from the question of monopoly, the small producer in many industries is handicapped in the presence of his large competitor. It should be remembered, however, that it was, for the most part, only in the production of cotton that this struggle could have been acute, for it was the practice throughout Georgia before the war to raise for home consumption such supplies as vegetables, wheat, corn and meat. To the extent that the small producer also raised these necessaries, he was in a position of independence.

The position of the small proprietor has been compared with that of the planter because there were many of these small farmers with holdings ranging in size from a few acres up to several hundred, and because it was easy for a person to acquire a small farm. Up to within a generation of the war the state practiced, as has already been pointed out, a liberal system of land distribution, and for several years after the last distribution, continued to encourage the acquisition of land by reducing the already low fees connected with the taking out of reverted grants.

Inasmuch as there were over 53,000 active farms in the state in 1860, it is fair to assume that about one-half of the white population of 580,000 had an immediate interest in the land. It is beyond the scope of this essay to attempt to give the economic status of the other half. Many were small shopkeepers and merchants in the towns and cities; some were doctors, lawyers, preachers and teachers; a few were tenants; some were mechanics and blacksmiths; some worked for wages in various capacities, and many were employed as overseers on plantations. It is true that many of them led a very precarious, hand-to-mouth existence. This, however, is not an exceptional phenomenon to be found only in slave societies; on the contrary, it seems to be universal in its manifestations.

Owing to the abundance of land in Georgia and to the profitableness of the plantation system in the production of cotton the large land holdings tended to increase in number and size. Owing to the abundance of land this tendency cannot be said to have made the economic struggle very hard before the war. Owing to the fact that there was a limit to the supply of land, and owing to the exploitative methods of cultivation, as well as to the natural increase of population, the tendency was toward an increased hardship for those less successful in the economic struggle.

After the above discussion which has proceeded upon the assumption of the effectiveness of the slavery-plantation system in cotton production and which has attempted to show that the system, while productive, was in Georgia at least, not so productive as to render precarious the condition of the small producer, it seems less than useless to adduce evidence for the purpose of showing that the system was really efficient. Still one of the great arguments brought against slavery as an economic institution was that since it offers no wholesome incentives to the laborers, their work is performed poorly and uneconomically. This is certainly true from an ideal point of view, regarding all peoples as being fairly well supplied with incentives and endowed with powers capable of making an adequate response to the incentives. It may happen, however, in the history of a race that the desire for improvement may operate so slightly that a distinct measure of progress may come from properly bringing to bear upon such a race so circumstanced artificial impelling stimuli. If a system can exact a degree of co-ordinated economic activity greater than would exist if natural inclination alone were operative, then the system, when applied under circumstances favorable to large-scale organized production, may not be so very bad as an engine of production. The opinion is ventured that far more goods for consumption were produced in Georgia before 1860 through the slavery-plantation system, than the same population would have produced had each worked independently for himself. Again, the assertion is ventured, that, although the slaves undoubtedly produced more than they consumed under the system, they consumed more than they would have produced outside the system.

All of this is said not so much in justification of slavery as it there existed, as in explanation of its persistent hold upon the people of the state. Herein, then, lies the explanation of the growth of large holdings in Georgia before the war: the abundance of land and the profitableness of the slavery-plantation plan of production.

CHAPTER II

TENDENCIES IN LANDOWNERSHIP AMONG THE WHITES SINCE THE WAR

EVERY one knows that the civil war gave the economic organization of the state a tremendous shock—as far-reaching in its effects as the jar of an earthquake upon a city. One influence of the jar was the cracking of the large plantations, from which fragments have been falling up to within recent years. Another effect was the liberation of a half million negro slaves whose relationship to the soil was thereby made to undergo a radical readjustment.

Connected with these problems, and as an outgrowth of the changed situation, several systems of tenancy were developed. The altered condition also invited the rise and extension of a plan of credit, which is a matter of great importance in studying the forces affecting the tenure of land. All of these problems are to be considered in order in the succeeding parts of this essay. It is the purpose of this chapter to present the extent and nature of the splitting up of large holdings, and to disclose the readjustment in the white ownership of land wrought out under the revised order of things, in so far as this can be done by the use of statistics.

Before entering into the discussion proper something should be said concerning the nature and amount of the land subject to ownership. The land surface of Georgia is larger than that of any other state east of the Mississippi. There are in the state approximately 59,000 square miles,[1] or over 37,700,000 acres of land. However, not all these acres are included in farms. The cities and towns take up a small percentage of the total area, cutting down to that extent the amount of land in farms. In the mountainous counties of the north, as well as in the timbered and pine barren counties of the south, there are vast tracts of land not brought as yet within the scope of farming operations. So that, according to the census, there are only 26,400,000 acres of land in farms in the state.[2] These figures indicate that the farms include only seventy per cent of the total acreage. Moreover only forty per cent of the seventy per cent, or twenty-eight per cent of the total, is reckoned as improved farming land.[3] Both of these percentages, however, run much higher in the main farming section of the state—that is to say, in the great body of central and southwestern counties. In these counties all except a little of the land is included in farms, and a comparatively large percentage of this farming acreage is catalogued as improved land. As an indication of the wide scope the census gives the term *improved acreage*, it is sufficient to say that it excludes from the category only the land not yet brought into utilization for farming purposes, together with the land once so utilized but now covered with trees or shrubbery. Put into economic language this means that the improved acreage connotes the land lying within the margin of cultivation. There is really very little or no land outside the margin of utilization in Georgia, although there is much land lying under such disadvantages either of fertility or of

[1] *Twelfth Census*, vol. i, p. xl.

[2] *Ibid.*, vol. v, p. 692.

[3] *Ibid.*, p. 693.

situation that it is not actually cultivated, nor will some of it be cultivated for many years to come. To the extent that lands are privately owned, that is to say, to the extent that they have value, they are theoretically within the margin of utilization, although they may not be cultivated. Of course such lands are held speculatively, and their value is therefore predicated upon a future potentiality. If there were free lands within the state, they and they alone would be beyond the margin of utilization.

In this chapter which is concerned with tendencies in the ownership of rural land no sharp distinction is to be made between land that is actually, and land that is only potentially, within the margin of utilization. The relative size of these two categories has an important bearing on the question of land valuation, and is a matter of significance in relation to certain developments that are to be described later. However, the statistics of ownership about to be given do not pertain to quite all the rural land in the state. In providing for the returns of land for purposes of taxation, Georgia makes a distinction between improved and wild lands. "Improved" as here used has a much wider connotation than as used in the census. It is here used as practically synonymous with farming lands, including, therefore, both the improved and unimproved lands of the census classification. And it includes slightly more, for according to the state comptroller-general's report, eighty-five per cent of the lands, or 31,000,000 acres, is returned as improved or farming lands.[1] The remaining fifteen per cent, that is, the wild lands, lies chiefly in the northern and southern counties of the state.

[1] *Compt.-Gen. Report*, 1903, p. 166.

Enough has been said to give a measure of definiteness to the figures that are to be used in this and succeeding chapters. The wild land just referred to is to be left out of account altogether. When the census figures are used, they will refer to the 26,400,000 acres of improved and unimproved lands in farms. Finally, on the question of ownership, where figures based on the tax returns are used, reference will be made to the 31,000,000 acres there classified as farming land.

No possible analysis of the figures contained in the decennial census reports will reveal the nature and extent of the movements in land proprietorship that have taken place in Georgia within the past generation. It is true these reports have created the impression that there has been a decrease in the size of holdings. As will appear later, the impression happens to be correct, but the figures usually relied upon as warranting the belief are altogether misleading as to the extent of the shrinkage in the acreage of holdings. The census statistics bearing on this subject are as follows:[1]

Year	Number of farms	Average size of farms in acres	Total number of acres in farms
1860	62,003	429.8	26,650,490
1870	69,956	338.0	23,647,941
1880	138,627	187.9	26,043,282
1890	171,071	147.3	25,200,435
1900	224,691	117.5	26,392,057

[1] *Twelfth Census*, vol. v, pp. 688, 962.

This showing leads to the conclusion that there was a trebling of the number of farms from 1870 to 1900, and that in average size there was during the same period a sixty-five per cent decrease. So far as relates to the ownership of land no great significance can be attached to these figures, inasmuch as they pertain to a classification of farms and not to the ownership of these farms. Since the census reckons the plots of land cultivated by tenants and croppers as separate and distinct farms, it is true that in many cases several farms are operated on land owned by one person. For instance, suppose a man owns 1,200 acres of land, which is cultivated by twenty-five croppers; in the census enumeration this land would go down as twenty-five distinct farms in perhaps the twenty to fifty acre group. It is evident, therefore, that the census figures throw no distinct light upon the important question as to whether the lands of the state are falling into the hands of the few or into the hands of the many.[1]

A résumé of figures given in detail in the appendix[2] presents the following view of tendencies in landownership among the whites for thirty-one typical counties of the state:

[1] The inadequacy of these census returns together with the impression that in his immediate neighborhood many holdings of land were very large and seemed to be growing larger, led the writer to go in search of trustworthy data bearing on the subject. Through the kindness of the comptroller-general of Georgia, Mr. Wm. A. Wright, he was allowed access to the manuscript tax digests of the various counties of the state kept in that gentleman's office at the state capital. The archives of this office contain an almost complete set of these tax returns for each county from 1873 (or '74) down to the present time. Through a two months' examination of the digests the figures tabulated in the appendix were obtained.

[2] *Infra.*

Year	Number of white owners	Percentage of increase	Number of acres owned	Average size in acres	Percentage of decrease
1873	17,255	. . . . .	6,734,398	388.6	
1880	20,725	20.1	7,036,536	339.5	12.7
1890	24,058	16	7,066,506	292.7	13.4
1902	26,957	12	7,138,586	264.8	9.8

It appears that there was a fifty-six per cent increase in the number of white landowners from 1873 to 1902, and that there was a decrease of thirty-one per cent in the average size of the proprietorships. It will also be observed that the rate of increase in the number of owners has not been uniform throughout the period. Using the percentages of increase given in the table as a basis for decennial percentages, it is found that from 1870 to 1880 the proprietorships increased twenty-nine per cent; from 1880 to 1890, sixteen per cent; from 1890 to 1900, ten per cent. This shows that the first decade after the war gave the largest increase in the number of owners, while the most recent decade gave only a ten per cent increase. Nor has there been a uniform rate of decrease in the average number of acres held by each owner. From 1870 to 1880 the decrease was eighteen per cent; from 1880 to 1890, thirteen per cent; from 1890 to 1900, eight per cent. The details connected with these general movements, as well as some points in explanation of them, are to be given later.

In the following table, wherein the holdings are classified in groups according to acreage, the information with regard to tendencies is more detailed:

	1	2	3	4	5	6	7	8	9	10
Year	Under three acres	3 and under 10	10 to 20	20 to 50	50 to 100	100 to 175	175 to 260	260 to 500	500 to 1000	1000 acres and over
1873 . .	37	99	97	817	2,006	4,069	3,053	3,437	2,303	1,337
1880 . .	111	179	187	1,331	3,084	4,924	3,597	3,685	2,327	1,300
1890 . .	223	317	376	1,862	4,152	6,052	3,889	3,782	2,231	1,173
1902 . .	338	444	575	2,644	5,251	6,754	4,027	3,840	2,044	1,038

It is found that in each of the first eight groups the number of holdings has increased with remarkable persistency from 1873 to 1902, though in each one the rate of increase has suffered a decrease throughout the period. That is to say, the rate of increase in each of the eight groups was much higher from 1870 to 1880 than from 1880 to 1890, and higher from 1880 to 1890 than from 1890 to 1900.

In the last two groups an opposite tendency has operated; there has been a decrease in the number of holdings falling within each, and the rate of decrease has tended to increase from decade to decade. An exception, however, is to be made in the case of the period 1873 to 1880 for the five hundred to one thousand acre group, which shows an increase in proprietorships. The downward movement was also slight in that period for the tenth group. Notwithstanding this slight decrease from 1873 to 1880 in the number of holdings containing over five hundred acres there was during the same period a very large increase in the number of holdings in each of the groups below five hundred acres.

It appears, therefore, that 500 acres may be regarded as a dividing line between tendencies. The explanation of the large increase from 1873 to 1880 on one side of this dividing line, while there was only a slight decrease on the other, lies in the fact that a considerable acreage passed over during the period from the category of "wild" to that of "improved" land. This increase is indicated in the number-of-acres-owned column given above,[1] where it is shown that from 1873 to 1880 there was an increase of over 300,000 acres in the thirty-one counties. This increased acreage of improved land made possible the increased number of holdings in the smaller groups, even while the larger holdings suffered only a slight diminution in numbers. This must not be taken to mean that the new land was itself diffused among the people, and that, therefore, the large plantations remained intact. Instead of this the correct view is that many of the large plantations were cut up into smaller holdings for others and the new lands became the large holdings. This conclusion is not only warranted by the logic of the situation, but also indicated by studying the changes in the number of holdings in individual counties between the two dates.[2]

The following table[3] shows the percentage of increase (+) or decrease (—) in the number of white holdings by groups from 1873 to 1902:

[1] *Supra*, p. 35. [2] *Cf.* Table in Appendix, *infra*.

[3] Based upon the figures given on page 36.

1	2	3	4	5	6	7	8	9	10
Under three acres	3 to 10	10 to 20	20 to 50	50 to 100	100 to 175	175 to 260	260 to 500	500 to 1000	1000 acres and over
+	+	+	+	+	+	+	+	—	—
813	348	492	223	161	65	31	11	11	22

The large percentages of increase in the first three groups lose some of their apparent significance when it is remembered that the base on which the percentage is calculated in each of these cases is very small. It is probable that about one-fifth of one per cent of the rural lands owned by the whites are in plots containing less than twenty acres each. As might be expected, it is in the immediate vicinity of cities like Atlanta, Macon, Augusta, Savannah and Columbus that these very small holdings tend to prevail, because it is there that truck-farming to supply the cities has been found profitable. However, as the figures indicate, there is a considerable sprinkling of these very small proprietorships all over the state. Although the percentages of increase give an exaggerated idea as to the extent of the movement, still the wholesome truth remains that these small proprietorships are on the increase. It should be added that the tendency represents an upward trend in the social scale rather than a downward movement. That is to say, those coming into possession of these small tracts are usually those who previously possessed no land rather than those who once held larger tenures which have been pressed into narrower limits through the operation of adverse circumstances.

More significance however is to be attached to the downward and lateral movements in the other columns, not only because they affect far more people but also because they pertain to the distribution of over ninety-nine per cent of the lands owned by the whites. In the columns from the fourth to the eighth inclusive, the increase in the number of holdings varied from 223 per cent to eleven per cent; or, considering these groups as a whole, there was an increase of sixty-seven per cent in the total number of white owners of land-tracts ranging in size from twenty to five hundred acres. These tracts represented in 1902 about fifty-two per cent of the total acreage owned by whites, whereas in 1873 the holdings ranging in size from twenty to five hundred acres represented slightly less than forty per cent of the total acreage.

In passing to the last two columns it is found that, whereas in 1873 they contained about twenty-one per cent of the owners and sixty per cent of the acreage, in 1902 they had about eleven per cent of the owners and forty-seven per cent of the land. A detailed statement of these percentages by groups and by dates is here presented:

	Year	Under 20 acres	20 to 50	50 to 100	100 to 175	175 to 260	260 to 500	500 to 1000	1000 acres and over
Percentage of total acreage falling in each group	1873	*	.5	2.5	8.0	9.0	20.	25.	35.
	1880	*	.7	3.5	9.8	11.	20.	25.	30.
	1890	0.1	1.0	4.7	12.2	12.	20.	24.	26.
	1902	0.5	1.5	6.0	13.0	12.	20.	22.	25.
Percentage of owners falling in each group	1873	1.4	4.7	11.6	23.6	17.7	20.	13.3	7.7
	1880	2.3	6.4	14.9	23.7	17.3	17.8	11.3	6.3
	1890	3.8	7.7	17.3	25.2	16.2	15.7	9.3	4.8
	1902	5.0	10.0	19.4	25.0	15.0	14.2	7.5	3.8

* Too small to estimate.

Mathematical exactitude is not claimed for the percentages just given. They do nevertheless come within a reasonable range of accuracy and trustworthiness, and a perusal of them easily leads to some interesting information touching the ownership of land in the state. A few of these facts not yet adverted to will be mentioned. Throughout the period covered by the figures a small percentage of the proprietors have owned a large percentage of the total acreage; for instance, in 1902 less than four per cent of the owners held one-fourth of the land, the holding of each containing over one thousand acres. In the beginning of the period something over one-half and at the end slightly less than one-half of the land was held in tracts containing over five hundred acres, while the number of holders of such tracts fell from a twenty-one per cent rank to an eleven per cent rank. This discrepancy between the two rates of percentage decline does not indicate an increase in the average size of these large holdings, but is to be explained by the fact that the crumbling of one large plantation suffices to give rise to many small proprietorships.

Again, especially noteworthy is the constancy with which the two hundred and sixty to five hundred acre tracts have held their relative rank. Throughout the period approximately one-fifth of the acreage has been in holdings varying in size from two hundred and sixty to five hundred acres. The one hundred to one hundred and seventy-five acre group shows the highest percentage of owners; for the period, approximately one-fourth of the owners held tracts in size between these two limits.

The most important general conclusion from the above table is that the percentage for both the acreage and the owners shows a downward movement to the left—a movement, however, not possessing the strength that has usually been attributed to it. Two opposing tendencies have operated with reference to the size of holdings—one to divide, the other to multiply it. Several forces have operated on the side of each of these tendencies. The figures go to show that the forces of diminution have prevailed slightly over the forces of increase. It is hoped that the next chapter will throw some light on the action of these opposing forces.

The figures thus far used in this discussion pertain only to thirty-one of the one hundred and thirty-seven counties in the state, but they have been used as warranting conclusions respecting the ownership of land among the whites throughout the state. This has not been an unfair procedure, because the counties to which the figures specially relate are representative counties.[1]

In order to get at the geographical distribution of holdings with respect to their size, and in order to get within the nearest range of exactness touching the number of landowners, as well as the average acreage per proprietorship for the state as a whole, a study was made of the 1903 tax digest (1902 digest used in four or five instances) for each of the one hundred and thirty-seven counties, with the results presented in the Appendix.[2]

[1] The following modification, however, is to be borne in mind in applying to the state the conclusions warranted by the statistics describing the thirty-one counties: There are four or five counties not represented in the above figures, that tend to reduce the average size of holdings throughout the state. These are the counties having a large city each —Fulton, with Atlanta; Bibb, with Macon; Muscogee, with Columbus; Richmond, with Augusta, and Chatham, with Savannah. In the vicinity of these cities many small truck farms have developed, and, although they represent an important phase of farming in Georgia, it was thought best to confine the above statistics to the strictly rural counties.

[2] *Infra.*

The table shows that there are 124,647 white owners of "improved" rural lands in Georgia, and that they own 29,769,720 acres. These figures indicate that the average size of white holdings is 238.8 acres.[1]

If a map of the state is drawn to show the average size of holdings in each county, and if those counties are shaded in which the average acreage of holdings is greater than the average for the state (238.8), it is found that all the shaded counties are in the southern and central parts of the state, whereas without a single exception in each of the northern counties the average size of holdings is below the average for the state.[2] It has always been the case that the holdings in the southern part of the state were larger than in the northern counties, while the middle counties have ranked in size, as well as in location, between the extremes, with a tendency for the holdings to be larger in the eastern section of this middle belt than in the western.

It should be remembered in this connection that most of the northern lands were distributed under the seventh and eighth lottery acts which provided for a partition of the land into lots of one hundred and sixty or forty acres each. In explaining the present existence of the smaller proprietorships in this region, this early distribution policy is a matter of some importance. Had the original grants been larger it is likely that the average size would

[1] According to the estimate based on the figures for thirty-one counties as given on page 35, the average size in 1902 was 264.8 acres. It is not to be inferred that there was so great a decrease in the average acreage of holdings from 1902 to 1903 as is here indicated. The discrepancy is explained, in part at least, by the fact that the calculations for 1903 include the city counties referred to in a former note (p. 41), while in the 1902 estimate these counties are not represented.

[2] See map in the Appendix, (*infra*).

now be much larger. The lots were made small primarily because it was thought that gold, copper, iron and other minerals were to be found there. While the full expectations in this regard failed of realization, there has been a noteworthy persistence of relatively small holdings, due to the fact that no great economic motive has operated to increase the acreage in the farms.

In the southern part of the state the grants were large, embracing sometimes four hundred and ninety acres; and although much of this southern territory has not yet been used for farming purposes proper, still an economic motive has operated to bring large tracts into the hands of the few as turpentine plantations and lumber farms. It is likely that exploitative methods are employed in both of these industries, and that they will tend to give way more and more to the cultivation of the soil, and this will lead to a greater subdivision of the land. Indeed, the statistics show that this has already begun.

It is a matter of interest to see whether the increase in the ownership of land among the whites has kept pace with the increase in the white population. In 1900, one out of every nine or ten white persons in the state owned some farming land. The owners stood in about the same numerical relation to the total white population in 1860. From 1860 to 1880, however, the owners of land increased faster than the population; in the next decade the two rates of increase were about the same; while from 1890 to 1900 the white population outran the increase in white proprietorships.[1] It appears, therefore, that now, as in 1860, about every other white family in Georgia owns land.

[1] These conclusions are based on population as given in the census and on the proprietorships as given in the Appendix.

As to localization within the state it may be said that in the region where the white population is less dense there the average size of holdings is largest, and there also the ratio between population and proprietorships is smallest. This is true of the great body of southern counties in the state.

It is hoped that the next chapter will bring into view some of the forces that have operated to effect changes in the ownership of land, and it is also hoped that subsequent parts of this monograph will throw some light on the varying relations which the owners sustain to the farming operations.

CHAPTER III

THE INFLUENCE OF THE CREDIT SYSTEM ON LANDOWNERSHIP

HAVING presented in some detail a statistical view of the tendencies at work for a generation among the white owners of land in Georgia, an endeavor will now be made to show some of the inner economic forces which serve to explain the above-mentioned tendencies, and which also reveal certain counter movements too elusive in nature to be detected in a general statistical survey.

The suddenness with which the slaves were made free and the consequent disorganized condition of labor prevented the immediate natural readjustment of the economic forces of the state. The large farmers who had prospered under the old régime were unable to adjust themselves to the new order of things so swiftly brought upon them. They were not only confronted by the necessity of making a new alignment of the productive forces, but they had to face the problem with greatly curtailed resources. The war had left them without money, and without any easy way of getting it. The farms were large, and the logic of the situation demanded the employment of the newly emancipated labor upon them. This labor just at this juncture was extremely mobile, though its movements were not in every case those of the "economic man." Out of these conditions, instead of the rise and development of a wage system of labor on the farms formerly worked by slaves, there arose tenancy and "cropping" arrangements which are to be described in some detail in subsequent chapters. The importance of the matter in this connection is, that all of these circumstances led to the development of a plan of agricultural credit of peculiar significance in its relation to land tenures in the state.

As early as December, 1866, a law was passed for the purpose of enabling those without money to get advances of supplies and other necessaries used in making crops. This act provided, in the first place, that landlords might have, by special written contract, a lien upon the crops of their tenants, for the stock, farming utensils and provisions furnished such tenants for the purpose of making their crops. It stipulated, in the second place, that factors and merchants might have a lien upon the growing crops of farmers, for provisions furnished and for commercial manures furnished, upon such terms as might be agreed upon by the parties.[1]

In 1873, the law relating to these liens was somewhat extended and made more specific in its details. The act of January, 1873, said:

> that factors, merchants, landlords, dealers in fertilizers, and all other persons furnishing supplies, money, farming utensils, or other articles of necessity to make crops, and also all persons furnishing clothing and medicines, supplies or provisions for support of families or medical services, tuition or school books, shall have the right to secure themselves from the crops of the year in which such things are done or furnished, as is now given by law . . . to factors and merchants.

Just as in the previous law it was provided that such liens must be created by special contract in writing. In

[1] *Acts of the General Assembly of the State of Georgia*, 1866, p. 141.

order that the person taking a lien might know to what extent the property was already encumbered, it was also provided that, if asked, the giver of the lien should give information on this point. The law declared that to give false information in such cases would operate to place the offender in the same category, as to punishment, with those fraudulently making a second deed. The liens hereunder created were

> declared to be superior in rank to other liens, except liens for taxes, the general and special liens of laborers, and the special lien of landlords, to which they shall be inferior, and shall as between themselves and other liens not therein excepted, rank according to date, and shall only exist as liens on the crop of the year in which they are made.[1]

This law, in its completeness, was in force only two years, for in 1874 an act was passed repealing it, except in so far as it relates to landlords.[2] So that for the past thirty years in Georgia only landlords have had the legal right to take liens on the growing crops. This legal separation of merchants from an immediate relation to a great body of the farmers, that is to say, to the tenants, is a matter of great concern as bearing upon the question of landownership.

A hasty perusal of these lien laws is apt to suggest the conclusion that they are of only slight significance as affecting the ownership of land, although it would be granted that they are of considerable importance in connection with a study of the farming interests of the state in general and of the tenancies there existing in particular.

[1] *Acts and Resolutions of the General Assembly of Georgia*, January, 1873, p. 43.

[2] *Acts of the General Assembly of Georgia*, 1874, p. 18.

This conclusion seems to be justified by the fact that the laws pertain only to the growing crops, and do not give a direct warrant for the transfer of a single acre of soil. This, however, is not an adequate view, for the laws have operated to center upon the landowner a large share of the burden of the supplying business. Or perhaps it is nearer the truth to say that the laws have merely given a legal sanction to an economic fact. Considerations of safety, or, more properly, considerations looking to a lessening of risks, have caused the merchant to make the landowners responsible not alone for supplies obtained for personal use, but also, in many cases, for the supplies furnished their tenants. In other words, landownership has been the avenue through which approach has usually been made to the merchants for advances of supplies.

So true is the analysis just given that in 1890 the practice there set forth was crystallized in a law enacted for the purpose of extending the scope of the landlord's special lien for supplies. Here it is declared that a special written contract is not required in order to create a landlord's supply lien, but that such a lien arises by the operation of law from the relation of landlord and tenant as well as by written contract, whenever the landlord shall furnish the tenant articles of necessity used in making the crop. Furthermore, and this is important as crystallizing the custom above referred to, the law said that whenever such liens are created by special contract in writing "the same shall be assignable by the landlords, and may be enforced by the assignees in the manner provided for the enforcement of such liens by landlords."[1] This puts a legal guarantee upon a transfer of the crop

[1] *Acts of the General Assembly of Georgia*, 1890–91, p. 72.

lien to the merchant. Moreover, in making this transfer the landlord usually becomes liable for the debt as endorser.

A farmer may usually secure a debt in one or more of three ways: he may give a real estate mortgage, he may give a chattel mortgage, he may give a mortgage on the growing crop. Of course the farmer would prefer to give only the latter, inasmuch as that brings into jeopardy only the year's income for the sake of the year's expenditures. Owing, however, to the risks of crop failure and the like, the merchant regards a prospective crop, considered alone, as a rather unsubstantial security for a debt. Nowadays this is very often combined with a chattel mortgage, that is, a mortgage on mules, cows, wagons and the like. In so far as those tenants are concerned who farm without the direct aid or intervention of landlords, only the last two forms of security can be used. The merchant prefers the real estate mortgage, and he was able up to within recent years to demand to a considerable extent such security. The forces which have contributed toward the freeing of the farmers from the necessity of mortgaging their acres, and towards the mitigation of some of the evils connected with the other two classes of mortgages, will be described later.

It is now desired to call attention to the influence which the land mortgages have had on the proprietorships. As suggested above, not alone were the farmers who cultivated their own acres brought within the scope of these mortgages, but also the owners of larger tracts who endorsed the accounts of their tenants with the merchants. A very acceptable form of endorsement in many cases was a "deed to secure debt, with power of sale." Such a mortgage was the occasion of the transfer of titles to much land in Georgia. Thus many large landed estates during the past generation were sliced and sliced until only a slice was left. In this way also many of the smaller farms were lost to their owners. And in this manner much land has come into the possession of merchants in the small towns. Of course not all the lands now owned by merchants were acquired from defaulting creditors, but an interestingly large percentage of their holdings was so acquired.[1]

The *Eleventh Census* (1890) undertook to shed some statistical light upon the question of real estate mortgages throughout the country. According to this investigation, 75,848 mortgages were recorded against 18,130,372 acres of land in Georgia during the decade from 1880 to 1890.[2] This was on the average about 7,500 covering 1,800,000 acres each year. This average means little, however, since there was a noteworthy increase from year to year throughout the period. In 1880, 3,353 mortgages covering 793,486 acres were made, while in 1889, 10,242 mortgages were made against 2,298,461 acres of ground.

Since many mortgages were never recorded, the figures represent inadequately the extent to which titles to land were jeopardized during the period. Of course, in some cases the mortgages instead of representing a jeopardizing of landholdings really indicated the reverse —that is to say, a mortgage sometimes marked the beginning of the acquisition of a farm. But in most

[1] It is estimated that in Coweta county—a typical cotton-raising county —fifteen per cent of the land is owned by merchants. This estimate is approximately correct, for a person knowing all the merchants of the county was generous enough with his time to consult the tax digest of the county and to tabulate the amounts of land returned by the merchants of the county.

[2] *Eleventh Census*, Real Estate Mortgages, p. 371.

cases the mortgage was not made to secure the purchase money, and hence it indicated a loosening rather than a tightening of the farmer's grip upon the soil.

Three of the one hundred and two counties receiving special investigation as to mortgages at the *Eleventh Census* were in Georgia. In these counties—Bartow, Houston and Twiggs—thirty-two per cent, forty-six per cent and sixty per cent respectively of the mortgages in force January, 1890, were for farm and family expenses.[1] These figures do not give an exaggerated view of the real situation. It is likely that these percentages would be somewhat larger if they had reference only to farm mortgages instead of to both farm and other real estate mortgages.

Even in those cases in which mortgages were made for farm and family expenses, it should be remembered that although titles to the land were thereby imperiled, a real change in ownership was not in every case effected. The mortgages were made to secure debts; they were executed therefore only in those cases in which the debts lapsed. These cases were numerous, however, on account of the decline in the price of cotton from 1874 to 1898, and also on account of the slowness with which the farmers have been adjusting themselves in accordance with the best combination of the productive factors. Again, it should be mentioned that in many cases the force of a mortgage was not required to effect a transfer of land. Some sold land in order to liquidate their indebtedness, although the merchants held no mortgages against the land.

All of this means that during the period under consideration the farmers of the state were as a rule not

[1] *Eleventh Census*, Real Estate Mortgages, p. 287.

prosperous. Most of them did not make any entrepreneur's profit; many of them not only failed to make normal returns to labor and capital, but even sank in the business much of the capital with which they began the period. This capital was sunk in two ways: one has just been described at considerable length; the other was in the nature of a decline in the value of the land.

Since 1898 the situation has materially improved. The farmers in general and the landowning farmers in particular are now in much better economic condition than they have been for many years—in fact their condition is better than it has been at any time since the war. Three important influences have contributed to the bringing about of this result: the Farmers' Alliance movement, the increase in the number of country banks, and the higher prices that have prevailed in the cotton market since 1898. These influences will be considered in the remaining parts of this chapter.

In order to appreciate the full significance of the Alliance movement it is necessary to refer again to the credit system for the purpose of directing attention to one aspect of it thus far not mentioned, although in reality it is the essential feature of the system, and has, therefore, played an important rôle in the breaking-up of the old plantations—a process whose outward manifestations were described in connection with the operation of the lien laws. Reference is made to the conspicuous difference between cash and "time" prices in the credit arrangement. It is this difference between cash and credit prices that has caused the system to bear so heavily on the farmers of the state. The procedure by which this comes about will now be described.

At the beginning of each year the farmer resorts to the merchant, with whom he negotiates for a line of credit, usually by signing papers in the manner above outlined in discussing the lien laws. Within this line of credit, limited in range according to the size of the farm, purchases of provisions, clothing, implements and other necessaries are made along from January to July or August. These lines of credit vary from sixty dollars up to one hundred and twenty-five dollars against a one-horse farm of from twenty to thirty acres, and from one hundred and twenty-five to two hundred and twenty-five dollars against a two-horse farm. When the negotiations are made at the beginning of the year, it is understood that the goods bought will be charged on the books not at competitive cash prices, but at time prices, though usually the ratio which the latter shall bear to the former is not the subject of any specific agreement between the parties concerned. As therefore from time to time purchases are made by the farmer, the goods are quoted to him at "time" prices, and nothing is said about the cash value of the articles. Inasmuch as many of the farmers are ignorant, and inasmuch as they can usually obtain credit with only one merchant at a time, it seems that the merchant is given an inviting opportunity for making undue exactions from the farmer in the matter of prices. Such is, indeed, the case, and without doubt many innocent and helpless farmers have become in this way the victims of unscrupulous merchants. But some writers have exaggerated not only the inclination, but also the power of the merchants in this regard. Of course in so far as the customer is ignorant, and is without friends capable of advising him, he is at the mercy of the merchant everywhere. The credit system merely enlarges the possibility of extortion in such cases. This fact, however, must not obscure the further fact that credit prices are also competitive prices.

Usually there are several merchants in each town competing vigorously for business. In case one merchant, after securing through a mortgage or otherwise the trade of a farmer, makes heavy exactions by means of excessively high credit prices throughout the year, the more alert of his customers, after being so dealt with, will negotiate the following year for lines of credit with other merchants. In this way standard credit percentages to be added to the cash prices are established for the staple commodities. These percentages are higher in some communities than in others owing to variations in local economic conditions. They are higher for some commodities than for others, owing to the varying circumstances that affect the commodities.

The last-mentioned fact suggests a thought or two as to the real nature of this credit business. From the standpoint of the merchant it is a loan of capital. All the goods in the merchant's store are capital goods. When the farmer buys any of these goods on credit he, in the act of buying, contracts for a loan of capital from the merchant, and from the funds arising out of this loan he buys one or both of two distinct classes of economic goods; that is to say, he buys either goods for consumption or goods for production or both. The one class of goods is bought for the purpose of directly satisfying wants; the other class is bought for the purpose of aiding in production, and thus of indirectly satisfying wants. Meat and shoes belong to the first class; wagons and plows belong to the second class. As a usual thing the credit percentage is smaller in the latter than in the former class, for the reason that, being more or less durable capital goods, they stand as a partial security for themselves and they easily produce a rent and a sinking fund.

The other class of loans out of which goods for consumption are bought, are predicated largely upon the product of labor, with land as a collateral security. The practice now under consideration comes nearer giving color to the doctrinal basis of the wages fund notion than does any other. Nevertheless close examination shows that the process does not directly involve even a temporary diminution of capital. This is explained by stating that the farmer does not consume in order that he may produce, but that he produces in order that he may consume. So true is this, that even under the credit system he normally produces before he consumes. The crop lien itself is essentially a recognition that this product has value in all stages of its development, from its inception to its completion. The crop lien gives the merchant a claim upon this increasing value, while it tends to enable the farmer to consume day by day the virtual product of his labor.

If there were no unusual risks connected with this farm supply business, and if the farmers were vigorously alive to their own interests, the percentages added to the cash prices would approach the normal rate of interest. But neither of these conditions has been sufficiently fulfilled in Georgia. The credit system working in the midst of such unfavorable conditions brings about an unsatisfactory distribution of the product, to which reference will again be made in the closing chapter. To predicate a loan upon a crop is a daring venture. Those who have fallen by the wayside engaged in such an undertaking show that unusual ability is required for success. Bearing in mind also the fact that during the two decades preceding 1894 cotton declined in price seventy per cent, while increasing in the rate of production perhaps not more than twenty-five per cent,[1] it at once appears that conditions during that period were not favorable for the reduction of credit percentages. So grievous did these burdens become for the farmers that in the later eighties and early nineties a conscious movement arose on their part for the purpose of liberating themselves from the severe exactions of middlemen in general and supply merchants in particular. This was the famous Farmers' Alliance movement, which had its origin somewhat earlier in states further west.

From one point of view this whole movement was a fiasco, for not one of the specific plans of co-operation for curtailing what seemed to be the exorbitant profits of the merchants was carried through to a successful accomplishment of its purpose. From another point of view the organization exerted a beneficent influence upon the farmers. Inasmuch as a detailed history of this movement would go far beyond the purposes of this monograph, it is only necessary here to indicate some of the prominent schemes by which the farmers sought to better their condition, and then to point out that although failing to work in practice, they did tend to benefit the farmers, and thus to check the flow of land into the hands of the merchants.

The most conspicuous of these practical undertakings for self-relief was the so-called Alliance stores. The importance of these shops lies in the fact that they were organized for the purpose of meeting the most serious difficulty in the situation, that is to say, they were to open an avenue of escape from the evils of the credit system. These stores were organized by issuing stock at five dollars a

[1] As a basis for this calculation see Latham Alexander & Co., *Cotton Movements and Fluctuations* (29th ed.), pp. 110, 111; and *Twelfth Census*, vi, pp. 424, 425.

share. The members of a lodge immediately interested were urged to take stock, and thus help support an institution destined, as was thought, to free them from the severe exactions of the merchants. Managers were placed in charge of these stores. A former manager of one of these Alliance stores writes in a personal letter substantially as follows: Managers urged all the stockholders to give good profits both for cash and on time, since the undertaking was a new venture, and the stockholders would share profits; after running a few years it was claimed that they would become strong enough to sell goods more cheaply than regular merchants. The managers were in many cases very shrewd business men, while the bulk of the stockholders possessed no mercantile experience; it was therefore easy for the managers to get the business in such a tangle that the stockholders were willing to lose what they had put in and sometimes more in order to get out.

These stores failed utterly in their specific endeavors. And in explanation it may be said that the very condition which invited the rise of these co-operative stores foredoomed them to failure. If these farmers were failing as farmers simply because they were unable to bring sufficient managing ability to the problem of farming even after a life-time of experience in that business, it is absurd to suppose that they were capacitated to succeed in the mercantile business.

Various other co-operative schemes were tried with varying degrees of success. There were the co-operative warehouses run for the purpose of enabling the farmer to hold his cotton until the best prices could be obtained for it. There were co-operative ginneries run in order to lessen the expense of preparing the cotton for the market after it was gathered. There was an energetic fight waged against the jute bagging trust for the purpose of lessening the expense connected with wrapping the bale for the market. So resolutely was this battle fought that for a year or two a large percentage of the cotton was wrapped in cotton bagging instead of jute. Then too a co-operative plan of buying fertilizers met with some success in the way of cheapening this article for the farmer.

These particular successes, however, were of minor importance as compared with the general stimulating effect of the whole movement. The agitation and interchange of ideas were educative in a high degree, and tended to make the farmers more alert in promoting their economic interests. As a result of it all, risks were somewhat lessened, and the farmers were enabled therefore to deal with the merchants upon better terms.

It was said above[1] that three influences in particular have contributed toward improving the condition of the farmers of the state. One of these influences, that, namely, of the Alliance movement, has been described. The second influence is the increase in the number of country banks in recent years. At the end of the year 1903 there were in Georgia two hundred and twenty-one chartered state banks besides the forty-six national and several private banks.[2] About one hundred and twenty-five of the state banks have been chartered since 1898, and a large percentage of them have been located in the small towns within easy reach of the farmers. These banks are proving to be of great service to the farmers, especially to the land-owning farmers, in liberating them from the credit system. Money is borrowed from these

[1] *Supra*, p. 52.

[2] *Annual Report of the Treasurer of Georgia*, 1903, p. 2.

banks usually on accommodation notes, and then the farmer approaches the merchant with cash in hand, and thus gets goods at the very lowest cash prices. The rate of interest paid the bank is considerably less than the rate arising from the difference between cash and credit prices of goods. The difference between the bank rate and the merchant rate does not necessarily indicate, as a superficial view might suggest, an amount of extortion practiced by the latter. This is true, because the bank runs less risk than does the merchant, a fact arising from two sources. Bank borrowing is itself a selective process, only the more alert farmers making use of the bank. In the second place, the generally alert farmer is more alert about his bank obligations than about any other. He knows there is to be no dillydallying in this matter; that the debt must be met on a certain day or something very unpleasant will happen. Such knowledge is a good thing—it acts as a spur to effort.

As an index of the service which these banks are rendering the farmers, as well as an index of the generally improved condition of the land-owning farmers of the state, it may be pointed out that perhaps between one-half and three-fourths of the loans of the small town banks are made to the farmers, and that about the same percentage of the deposits is now to the credit of the farmers.[1]

[1] Mr. W. S. Witham, who is president of nearly fifty of these country banks in Georgia, addressed a letter on November 10, 1904, to the presidents of the several southern State Bankers' Associations proposing a plan by which the banks might in a concerted way enable the farmer to hold and market his cotton advantageously. One paragraph in this letter is interesting in this connection. He says: "The objection urged is, a farmer cannot afford to hold his cotton and must sell to pay his debts. In answer to this I will say that the farmer in the south is now in better financial condition than ever before, and in the forty-eight

The benefits coming from the banks inure primarily to the land-owning farmers rather than to the tenants and croppers. The landlords who usually stand security for the mercantile accounts of their tenants, and always of their croppers, have been enabled in recent years to obtain money from the banks, and with it to discount the monthly bills of their tenants and croppers with the merchants. This works to transfer the reward for risk-taking to the farmer. As an outcome of it all, the element of risk has been lessened, and even the tenants and croppers have reaped some benefits from the improved conditions. Although still suffering under the credit system it does not weigh so heavily upon them as in former times. In some cases credit percentages are fifty per cent and in many cases they are at least twenty-five per cent lower than they were fifteen years ago.[1]

'Witham Banks' in Georgia more than two-thirds of the money on deposit belongs to the farmers as against all other professions and depositors." The entire letter may be found in the *Atlanta Constitution*, December 13, 1904.

[1] The writer is well acquainted with an interesting case in Coweta county. It is by no means typical but it does show how the banks have enabled one farmer to display a very benevolent disposition toward his croppers. This farmer employs about fifteen or twenty croppers, some white and some black, agreeing to let them have a given amount of money each month to be used as they see fit, for which they are charged eight per cent interest (previous to 1904 he charged ten per cent). The farmer gets the money from the banks at a rate slightly less than this. He gives personal direction to the work of the croppers and as a consequence they produce at least fifty per cent more than the average croppers. It has been the policy of this farmer never to retain for another year a cropper who fails to "pay out" at the end of a given year. They rarely fail to "pay out," and usually have considerable cash in hand at the end of the year—results due in large measure to the efficient management under which they work. This is by no means a typical plan. There is in it a large measure of benevolence as is evidenced by the fact that croppers, both white and black, are eager to come to this plantation, and by the further fact that any cropper on the plantation,

The third great influence that has worked for the betterment of the farmers has come through the higher prices that have obtained in the cotton market since 1898. It was inevitable that this change should come unless far-reaching economies had been devised in the production of the staple. For there can be no doubt but that for several years in the nineties much of the cotton was sold for less than the cost of production. It does not require any very acute analysis to show that this condition could not last long, nor is it any more difficult to see that it was necessary for the change to be wrought out through the action of self-interest in the individual farmer. The world did not have too much cotton, it cannot have too much, but the farmer had produced too much, and he may do so again too.

During the past half-dozen years cotton has brought over twenty-five per cent more per pound than in the preceding half-dozen years. This has enabled most of the farmers in the state to cancel all debts. These higher prices have redounded to the benefit of the tenants and croppers, as well as to the independence of the landlords. It is perhaps true that these farmers are now (1904) at or near the top of a peak of prosperity, and that just ahead is a valley, but one not so dark and gloomy as that out of which they have come in recent years. The sixth chapter undertakes to point out the highways along which fundamental economic law is destined to lead the farmers of the state.

whether white or black, would rise any hour in the night and go through any sort of weather to the nearest town (seven miles away) in order to serve the man who thus plans so unselfishly for his well-being; and he would do this without expecting any specific reward for the particular errand.

CHAPTER IV

THE GENESIS AND DEVELOPMENT OF LANDOWNERSHIP AMONG THE NEGROES

BAD as was the economic condition of the whites in the South at the close of the civil war, that of the freedmen was even worse. In Georgia there were 500,000 of these recently liberated negroes, and this number embraced forty-five per cent of the entire population of the state. The swiftness with which they were led to make their flight from slavery into freedom left no time for the collection of any property on the way. It may be said, therefore, that in 1865 this considerable body of the state's citizenry possessed neither homes nor lands, and only slight traces of other forms of property. As individuals emerging from slavery they cannot be held answerable for their poverty.

Theretofore, as slaves they had been a factor in production and consequently a factor in distribution. It so happens, however, that under a régime of slavery the part of the product imputable to labor falls into the possession of the one who owns the laborer; just as under a régime of private landownership the part of the product imputable to the land is claimed by the owner of the land. If, however, the minimum of subsistence law of wages be true, the slaves were getting their normal economic share of the product, inasmuch as they were well provided for in respect to shelter, raiment and food. It may be questioned whether they would have produced outside the organization of slavery as much as they consumed within the system. Notwithstanding this, the fact remains that under the system of slavery, as it existed in Georgia, the negroes produced more than they consumed. The proof and extent of the fact are expressed in the value of the slaves. The product of a slave over and above his subsistence was capitalized into his selling value. Emancipation dissipated such values. Thus was left in the state only such wealth as was due to the other factors in production, and this that was left suffered a decrease in value owing to the breaking-up of the co-ordinated system of production. If the slaves had passed gradually into freedom they would doubtless have carried with them considerable amounts of property.

Although these negroes possessed no more property in 1865 than when they were transferred to the American soil generations before, they had received a training in industry and civilization that placed them several centuries ahead of their kinsmen left to develop in the original habitat. Starting with the assumption that in 1865 the negroes owned not an acre of land, it is the purpose of this chapter to ascertain with what degree of success they have brought this training to bear in the acquisition of farms.

By 1874 the negroes had acquired taxable titles to 338,769 acres of land in Georgia.[1] The geographical

[1] *Report of the Comptroller-General of Georgia* for 1874, pp. 58-63. Georgia soon after the war adopted the policy of keeping the returns of property made by negro tax-payers separate and distinct from the returns of the whites. This was a fortunate provision since it has placed within reach a valuable supply of material that serves as an index of the progress the negroes have made in the acquisition of property. Especially important are these returns in relation to the matter of negro landownership. For, however unreliable such a source of information may be in regard to other forms of property and even touching the value of

distribution of these holdings by counties is interesting, not only because it suggests the influences that operated in their acquisition, but also because it indicates in a rough way the main area within which the negro was to get his largest grip upon the soil during the succeeding thirty years.

In every county of the state, excepting Fannin, Union and Warren, the negroes had acquired either absolute or tentative titles to at least a few acres of land. The main body of their holdings, however, was south of a line extending from Columbus through Macon to Augusta. Of the sixteen counties containing over 5,000 acres each of negro-owned land, all, except one, were south of this line. Furthermore, as adding emphasis to the same point, it should be said that of the forty-five counties in each of which the negroes owned over 2,500 acres, only thirteen were to the north of the line. Since the counties in the south are larger than elsewhere in the state, it is possible that an absolutely larger acreage per county in the possession of negroes might not indicate a relative ascendency of negro holdings in those counties. But when the negro acreage considered in relation to the total county acreage is compared in the two sections of the state, the fact is established that the negroes owned a considerably larger percentage of the lands south than of those north of the above-mentioned line.

A map constructed to show this localization of negro holdings reveals two main centres of development: the one, in the southeastern part of the state beginning at

land, it nevertheless supplies data concerning the acreage of land-holdings that come within a reasonable range of accuracy and trustworthiness. Since 1874, the comptroller-general has published in his annual reports a statement of the number of acres of land returned for taxation by the negroes in each of the counties of the state.

the coast and extending inland across about three tiers of counties;[1] the other, in the southwestern part of the state. The rise of the first and more important of these centers of negro landownership may be explained as the logical outcome of the situation in the region immediately after the civil war. This struggle caused a greater disorganization of the economic forces in the six seaboard counties than elsewhere in the state. In antebellum days these counties were distinguished for their large plantations, and for the large number of slaves worked upon them in the cultivation of rice and sea-island cotton. Excepting Chatham, the county in which Savannah is located, the average number of slaves per slave-holder in this region in 1860 was twenty, while the average for the state was about eleven. In these six counties were to be found more than one-fourth of all the slave-holders owning over one hundred slaves each. The war utterly destroyed the foundations underlying the prosperity of these planters.

An Englishman residing on one of these plantations described the situation in a letter written to a friend in England in the early seventies. He says that these rice plantations were originally reclaimed and afterwards maintained at great expense of labor, because of the levees, *etc.*, that had to be kept up; owing to the lack of capital and labor since the war much of this country had returned to its original condition. After quoting statistics to show the great decrease in rice production, he continues:

The original planters having been completely ruined by the war, the planting in many cases has been carried on by negroes

[1] The counties in the region of the Okefinokee swamp must be excepted.

on their own account in small patches. As the Agricultural Commissioner, in his report, has lately stated—" The rice planters were driven from the Carolina and Georgia shores during the war, labor was in a disorganized and chaotic state, production had almost ceased, and at its close, dams, flood-gates, canals, mills and houses were either dilapidated or destroyed and power to compel the laborers to go into the rice swamps utterly broken. The laborers had scattered, gone into other businesses, and those obtainable would only work for themselves on a share contract. . . . ." This picture is by no means overdrawn and even now, in our own neighborhood, there is scarcely a planter whose plantation is not mortgaged and whose crop is not the property of his factor who had advanced him money to plant with. They plant on sufferance, and live from hand to mouth as best they can.[1]

Another acute observer of conditions in these counties declared that, immediately after the war, most of the planters were utterly ruined, not having money enough to buy food for their own families, and that most of the finest plantations were lying idle for want of hands to work them.[2]

It was in the midst of this chaotic condition of things that the negroes began to acquire tracts of land. After a few years of experimenting most of the planters who were able to operate their rice farms at all adopted the plan of paying the negroes wages, instead of renting to them on shares. On this point one of these planters writes about 1878:

We all pay wages either weekly or monthly, finding that the best plan now. It is easy for ourselves and satisfactory for

[1] Frances Butler Leigh, *Ten Years on a Georgia Plantation since the War*, London, 1883, pp. 263, 264.

[2] *Ibid.*, pp. 15, 24.

the negroes who can't think they are cheated when everything is paid in full every Saturday night, nor can they forget in that short time what days they have been absent or missed work.[1]

The plan of paying wages enabled some of the more alert and ambitious negroes to take advantage of the cheapness of land and buy farms for themselves. For instance, at the close of the year 1867 on one of these plantations $6,000.00 were paid in cash as wages to the negroes employed on it, many of them getting as much as $200.00 or $300.00 each. The complaint is made that as a result of this policy many of the negroes left the plantation in order to buy land for themselves.[2] In some cases they bought these lands from irresponsible persons, secured no titles and consequently were soon driven off. Sometimes they bought on the instalment plan, but failing to make the necessary payments they had to surrender their claims. But there were other cases in which the negroes came into absolute possession of considerable tracts of land.

Nor was it in the counties of the coast alone that they acquired farms. In reality by 1874 they owned more land in the six counties to the northwest of the seaboard counties than in the latter. This is explained by the fact that coincident with the downfall of the rice plantations there was a great migration of the negroes from the coast to the interior counties. In these neighboring interior counties the population was sparse, and there was an abundance of wild land obtainable at low rates. In their flight, therefore, many of the negroes found permanent homes and acquired lands in this region.[3]

[1] Leigh *op. cit.*, p. 226. [2] *Ibid.*, p. 79.

[3] The statistical revelation on the subject finds confirmation from a

The other center of negro landowning, as stated above,[1] was in the southwestern corner of the state. In this section before the war large plantations were being built up, and the negroes were beginning to outnumber the whites. There were vast stretches of wild land still untouched in those counties when the negroes became free. With the breaking-up of the system upon which the prosperity of the plantation rested, it was natural that a few of the more sanguine negroes should come into possession of some of these easily obtainable lands.

Thus the two chief centers of negro landownership have been located—the one in the southwestern, the other in the southeastern part of the state; the one in a region where the negroes outnumber the whites, the other in a region where the whites outnumber the negroes;[2] each in a region where the density of population is below the average density for the state, the one being in a region slightly below, the other in a region greatly below this average. Both of them therefore were in regions of relative land abundance where the economic struggle was less acute. Some of the causes leading to such a localization have been mentioned. It now remains to trace the course of development from the small beginnings found in 1874, to weigh the real significance of the movement, and to point out the forces that seem to hinder a larger increase in landownership among the negroes.

The following table shows the acreage owned by negroes in Georgia by years from 1874 to 1903, and also

rice planter who writing in 1870 said: "Many negroes left to settle on their own properties in the pine woods." Leigh, *op. cit.*, p. 155.

[1] *Supra*, p. 65.

[2] This region, however, is in close proximity to the seaboard counties in which the negroes outnumber the whites.

the percentages of increase or decrease from year to year:[1]

Year	Number of acres owned by negroes	Percentage: Of increase or decrease	Percentage: Cumulative	Year	Number of acres owned by negroes	Percentage: Of increase or decrease	Percentage: Cumulative
1874 .	338,769	. .	27	1889 . .	877,112	0.9	70
1875 . .	396,658	17.8	32	1890 . .	967,234	10.2	77
1876 . .	457,635	15.3	37	1891 . .	1,004,306	3.8	80
1877 . .	458,999	0.2	37	1892 . .	1,063,649	5.9	85
1878 . .	501,890	9.3	40	1893 . .	1,043,860	—1.8	83
1879 . .	541,199	7.8	43	1894 . .	1,064,431	1.9	85
1880 . .	586,664	8.4	47	1895 . .	1,038,824	—2.4	83
1881 . .	660,358	12.5	53	1896 . .	1,043,847	0.4	83
1882 . .	692,335	4.8	55	1897 . .	1,057,567	1.3	84
1883 . .	666,583	—3.7	53	1898 . .	1,097,087	3.8	87
1884 . .	756,703	13.5	60	1899 . .	1,062,223	—3.0	85
1885 . .	788,376	4.1	63	1900 . .	1,075,073	1.2	86
1886 . .	802,939	1.8	64	1901 . .	1,141,135	6.1	91
1887 . .	813,725	1.3	65	1902 . .	1,175,291	3.9	94
1888 . .	868,501	6.7	69	1903 . .	1,251,714	6.4	100

From 1874 to 1884 there was an increase of one hundred and twenty-six per cent in the amount of land owned by negroes; from 1884 to 1894 the increase was forty per cent; from 1894 to 1903 the increase was seventeen per cent. Or, to consider other periods, from 1874 to 1880 the increase was seventy-three per cent; from 1880 to 1890 it was sixty-four per cent; from 1890 to

[1] Based on the figures given in the annual reports of the comptroller-general. For some of the figures see Du Bois, *The Negro Landholder of Georgia*, published in Bulletin No. 35, of Department of Labor, p. 665. Du Bois's monograph contains many interesting facts regarding the ownership of property among the negroes of Georgia.

1900 it was eleven per cent; from 1900 to 1903 it was sixteen per cent. Or, for the periods just named, the annual average rates of increase were respectively twelve per cent, six per cent, one per cent and five per cent. Or, to view the problem from still another standpoint in 1874, the negroes owned one in every eighty-five acres of improved land in the state; in 1880, they held one in every fifty; in 1890, one in every thirty-one; in 1900, one in every twenty-eight; in 1903, one in every twenty-five. These figures show that there has not been a uniform rate of increase during the past thirty years. On the whole, the rate of increase has suffered a decrease during the period, but even this decrease has been far from regular. From 1874 to 1892 there was some uniformity in the enlargement of the acreage owned by negroes, the most noteworthy perturbation being that in the early eighties, due no doubt to the general depression which then occurred augmented by the poor cotton crop of 1881. The years from 1892 to 1900 are marked by fluctuations in the amount of land held by negroes, with only a slight increase in the acreage taking the period as a whole—in fact there was not a two per cent increase from 1892 to 1900. It will be remembered that most of those years belong to the period of depression which bore with particular severity upon the farmers of Georgia, because of the abnormally low price of cotton then prevailing.

Since 1900 there has been a significant increase in the acreage—significant not so much because of the amount as because of the fact of the increase after eight years of arrested development.

Maps drawn to show the localization of these holdings for 1880, 1890, 1900 and 1903 indicate that the negroes have continued to maintain a stronger hold on the soil in the southwestern and southeastern counties of the state. These two centers have enlarged, and the counties which lie between them have also shown a relatively large increase, so that now practically all the counties south of the line extending from Columbus to Augusta, with the exception of those in the neighborhood of the Okefinokee swamp, form a region in which the negroes have been more successful than elsewhere in the state in the matter of acquiring farms.

It should be noted, however, that many of the central counties show a rate of increase in negro acreage since 1900 greater than the rate for the state as a whole. The same period gives also a large percentage of increase in most of the southwestern counties, whereas many of the southeastern counties show only a small rate of increase. This may be a very hopeful sign, indicative either of the increase in economic power on the part of the negro or of the growth of a more favorable economic environment, or both. For it indicates an increased acquisition of land in those parts of the state where the population is largest and the economic activity greatest. The parts just referred to form the main cotton-raising area of the state. It, therefore, appears that the high price of cotton in recent years has been the chief influence contributing to the acquisition of farms by the negroes. This is encouraging, as showing that some members of the race take advantage of such an opportunity by planning for a permanent future income instead of an immediate gratification.

Another fact is of importance in this connection. The development of cotton manufacturing in Georgia now in progress tends to increase the economic importance of the negro farmers.

Thus far no account has been taken of the tendencies

in regard to the size of negro holdings.[1] The following table gives a résumé of the figures on negro proprietorships for thirty-one counties as presented in detail in the appendix:

	1873	*1880*	*1890*	*1902*
Under three acres	18	100	371	690
3 to 10	39	131	579	760
10 to 20	19	154	372	713
20 to 50	88	434	678	1,068
50 to 100	107	451	664	883
100 to 175	130	327	444	619
175 to 260	78	180	242	276
260 to 500	29	69	116	153
500 to 1000	6	17	39	50
1000 acres and over	0	2	5	9
Total number of owners	514	1,865	3,510	5,221
Total number of acres	58,556	174,940	249,469	336,216
Average size of holdings	113.9	98.3	71.0	64.3

This table shows the average size of negro holdings to be sixty-four acres, which is, as would be expected, very much smaller than the average acreage of white holdings. It is seen also that negro holdings on the average have tended to grow smaller in size, just as throughout the same period there has been a decrease in the average size of white proprietorships. In the latter case, however, the decreased size was brought about by a multiplication of the smaller holdings at the expense of the larger ones, whereas in the case of the negroes there has been an increase in the number of large as well as small holdings, though the latter have increased faster

[1] Neither the census of the United States nor the reports of the comptroller-general of the state throw any light on this subject. Just as in the case of the ownership of land among the whites, information was obtained from the county tax digests. Thirty-one counties were investigated for the years 1873, 1880, 1890 and 1902, and the negro holdings were classified according to acreage as presented in the Appendix, below.

than the former—a fact explaining the decrease in average size.

The greatest increase has been in the number of those possessing less than twenty acres each. In 1902 forty-one per cent of the negro landowners held plots containing less than twenty acres, and in two-thirds of these plots the acreage was less than ten. On the other extreme it is found that only slightly over one per cent of the negro owners possess over five hundred acres each. Again, nearly one-half of the negro owners hold between twenty and one hundred and seventy-five acres. The most interesting of all the groups, as perhaps representing an ideal proprietorship, is the one embracing holdings ranging in size from twenty to fifty acres. In the classification adopted more negro landowners are found in this than in any other group. It contains about one-fifth of the total negro proprietors in the state.

It is now in order to point out the real significance of the above showing, touching negro landownership in its relation to the total acreage of the state. In 1903 there were 18,700 negroes owning land in Georgia,[1] that is to say, less than two per cent of the negroes held titles to farms. To be more exact, the figures indicate that only one negro in every fifty-five owns a farm, or only one holding in every six or seven is in possession of a negro. This is certainly no flattering showing for more than a generation's development, especially when it is remembered that forty-one per cent of these holdings contain less than twenty acres each.

A consideration of the total number of acres owned by the negroes in relation to the total acreage of the state but serves to emphasize the same fact. In 1903 the

[1] *Cf.* Appendix, *infra.*

negroes returned for taxation 1,251,714 of the 31,013,973 acres of improved land in the state,[1] that is, they own four per cent of the total farming area, or one in every twenty-five acres. Thus it is seen that while the negroes compose nearly one-half of the population (46.7 per cent), they possess only one twenty-fifth of the land. This is assuming that the lands returned for taxation are unincumbered. Without doubt many of these farms are mortgaged either to former owners because bought on the instalment plan or to merchants for supplies furnished. But granting that the titles are clear to all the land the tax digests attribute to them, the fact remains that the negroes have not become masters of much land in Georgia.

Mention has already been made of some of the forces which seem to explain the early localization of negro holdings. These influences were presented as being aids to land acquisition rather than otherwise. It now remains to refer to the forces that have operated to hinder the negroes from coming into possession of a larger share of the farming lands. These forces are to be found, first, in the psychological organization of the negro, and secondly, in his environment.

The first of these causes is, of course, the more fundamental. The typical negro is improvident; he does not make plans for the future and organize his present forces for the execution of the plans. The acquisition of a farm means the immediate consumption of less than is produced. If it be the disposition of any people to consume up to the limits of production, or, to state the same thing from another point of view, to produce only up to the demands of immediate consumption, then it

[1] *Report of the Comptroller-General of Georgia* for 1903, pp. 202, 166.

could only be through the operation of some fortuitous combination of circumstances that such a people should come into the possession of land. The average negro is not so psychologically organized as to defer a present gratification for the sake of a permanent future income.[1]

This lack of economic foresight, which is characteristic of the average negro, is the psychological product both of heredity and of training. So far as information is obtainable, there is no evidence to show that the ancestors of the American negro in the original habitat were accustomed to act under the influence of highly wrought economic motives. There is, however, an abundance of evidence to the contrary.[2] Now slavery, while improving in many ways the economic condition of the negro, did not possess the virtue of subjecting him to a training in providence. It was not incumbent upon him under the system to consider at all the matter of providing for his own economic welfare in respect to even such primary wants as food, clothing and shelter. In view of these antecedents in blood and training, and in view of the further fact that the other half of the population, originally in possession of all the land, is composed of descendants of a race distinguished for its individual enterprise and economic foresight, it is therefore not surprising to find that the negroes, while numbering

[1] A personal letter from Georgia, dated November 1, 1904, contains the following passage pertinent to the subject in hand: "This is certainly a prosperous year for the southern negroes. They have paid their accounts and have money to burn. Numbers of them have already received over $100.00 and they are spending it as fast as they get it." This has all the more force since it was not written in answer to an inquiry on that particular subject.

[2] *Cf.* Tillinghast, *The Negro in Africa and America* (1902), *Publications of American Economic Association*. Also Kelsey, *The Negro Farmer* (1903), pp. 22, 23.

about one-half of the population, possess only one-twenty-fifth of the land in the state.

This leads to the consideration of the extent to which the environment of the negro is unfavorable to his acquiring land. In the first place, no doubt there has been a disposition on the part of some white landowners to discourage the acquisition of land by negroes to the extent of refusing to sell to them on the simple ground that a negro, being a negro, has no business to own land. One would expect that the greater economic competition between the two races would tend to increase this feeling. The feeling, however, in its beginning was not a product of the economic struggle. It had its birth in the period of the reconstruction orgies, and as the vision of the negro's political dominion supported by the strong arm of the national government has vanished, it has become possible for the southern white man to take a saner attitude toward the negro as a citizen as well as an industrial factor. So that now, in Georgia at least, the attitude of the typical white landowner is not one that would dictate a refusal to sell land to a negro because of his color, nor would the color of the purchaser alter in any wise the terms upon which the land might be obtained.

Another influence of the environment that has undoubtedly worked to hinder the negroes in purchasing lands has been the generally unprosperous condition of the farmers up to within recent years. It is particularly noticeable that during the depression of the nineties, as was said above,[1] the negroes made little progress in acquiring farms. As will be discussed in another connection, many of the negro farmers are croppers upon

[1] *Supra*, p. 70.

cotton plantations, and owing to the shortcomings of the cropping arrangement, together with the credit system and the declining price of cotton up to 1898, they had little or no surplus left over at the end of the year. In so far, however, as lands in Georgia have been abundant—and they have been relatively abundant—the opportunity has been favorable for the enterprising and thrifty negro to become the owner of a farm.

A word should be said touching the status of those negroes who do cultivate farms of their own. They of course represent the most substantial element in the race, and, as a usual thing, are respected alike by the whites and the members of their own race. They obtain goods from merchants upon as good terms as do white men similarly circumstanced, and their complexion has no influence upon the rate of interest. They live in better constructed and better furnished homes, and on the whole make conservative citizens. The hope of the race seems to center in this element of the population. It is, therefore, to be hoped that the next few generations will see a large increase in the number of those possessing sufficient energy and thrift to acquire farms.

CHAPTER V

THE SYSTEMS OF FARMING BASED ON THE RELATION OF THE FARMER TO THE SOIL

THUS far attention has been directed to the distribution of lands among the people of the state from the point of view of ownership. It is the purpose of this chapter to describe the leading characteristics of the several other forms of land tenure that have been developed in Georgia since the war and to disclose some of the forces which will in a measure explain their rise, their extension and their retention. In the next chapter an attempt will be made to analyze the inner economic workings of these various plans of land tenure as systems of production and distribution.

By recalling the condition in which most of the landowners and freedmen found themselves immediately after the war, it is not difficult to understand the rise of what is called the "cropping" plan of farming. Rarely does it happen that an arrangement can be so easily and surely explained as the product of the existing economic situation. The landowners had no capital except land and the freedman lacked even land. Some landlords on the strength of their credit, which stood high in ante-bellum days, adopted the plan of working their plantations with hired laborers. However, the conditions of the moment were unfavorable to the success of this arrangement, inasmuch as the negroes, just liberated, naturally felt disposed to experience the joys of unhindered movements.

Unfortunately, however, their movements were made, for the most part, in response to a political motive externally suggested rather than in answer to a genuine economic motive internally inspired. It was often the case when wages were paid weekly or monthly that the laborers made weekly or monthly changes of location. These labor uncertainties tended to discredit the wages system even in those cases where the planters were in position to adopt it. Therefore, these three circumstances, namely, the landlord's scarcity of capital, the negro's poverty, and the negro's uneconomic mobility, combine to explain the rise of the cropping arrangement now to be described.

The cropping system, as it is called in Georgia, is a species of what economists call metayage. The essential features of the system as developed in Georgia are these: the landlord furnishes the land, house, live stock, farming implements and seed;[1] the cropper plants, works and gathers the crop; the crop is then divided equally between the landlord and the cropper; in case commercial fertilizers are used, this expense is borne in common, as is also the expense of ginning the cotton and wrapping it for the market. This arrangement arose out of the above outlined situation. It met the negro's lack of capital and acted as a steadying influence upon his migratory disposition.

Another outgrowth of the whole situation and adjunct to the system was the credit arrangement already described. In view of the landlord's depleted resources, it was necessary for him to negotiate for lines of credit on the basis of which he might equip his farm with the necessary stock and implements, and supply his croppers

[1] Sometimes the landlord furnishes only one-half of the seed.

with the necessary provisions. Sometimes these advances were secured from cotton factors, especially by those planters in the neighborhood of cities like Augusta and Savannah. By far the more important body of these credits soon came to be obtained from local merchants throughout the cotton belt of the state. It was, therefore upon the basis of the landlord's security that the croppers obtained such necessaries as food and clothing from the neighboring village merchant.

Before proceeding to point out the extent to which the cropping system has tended to prevail, it will be helpful to describe another plan of share distribution also practiced in the state, and to indicate the marks which serve to distinguish the one from the other. Reference is made to the "third and fourth" system, so called from the fact that the renter pays the landlord one-third of the grain and one-fourth of the cotton grown on the land which the latter supplies. In this tenure the landlord supplies only the land and house, while the tenant furnishes all other forms of capital as well as the labor required in the production of the crop. Moreover, the landlord is supposed to exercise far less supervision in the case of the "third and fourth" renter than in the case of the cropper.

It thus appears that the landlord in the cropping system is the chief manager and exclusive capitalist, and the cropper is, for the most part, only a laborer; whereas in the "third and fourth" plan the tenant is chief manager and capitalist, and the landlord is capitalist directly only to the extent of the value of the land supplied the tenant.

This distinction seems to underlie an opinion of the state supreme court rendered as early as 1872. The court said:

There is an obvious distinction between a cropper and a tenant. One has a possession of the premises, exclusive of the landlord; the other has not. The one has a right for a fixed time; the other has only a right to go on the land to plant, work and gather the crop. The possession of the land is with the owner as against the cropper. This is not so of the tenant. The case made in the record is not the case of a tenant. The owner of the land furnished the land and the supplies. The share of the cropper was to remain on the land and to be subject to the advances of the owner for supplies. The case of the cropper is rather a mode of paying wages than a tenancy. The title to the crop subject to the wages is in the owner of the land. We are of opinion, that no person can purchase or take a lien on the wages of the cropper, to wit: his share of the crop, until the bargain be completed, to wit: until the advances of the planter to the cropper for supplies, have been paid for. A different rule might obtain, as to a tenant, the right of the landlord being only a lien. But the cropper's share of the crop is not his until he has complied with the bargain.[1]

In 1888 the court reiterated this view when it said, "Where an owner of land furnishes it with supplies and other like necessaries, keeping general supervision over the farm, and agrees to pay a certain portion of the crop to the laborer for his work, the laborer is a cropper," and differs, therefore, in important respects from a renter.[2] The same view seems to form the basis of an act passed by the legislature of the state in 1889 for the purpose of making certain regulations respecting the relation of landlord and cropper. It was enacted that

whenever the relation of landlord and cropper exists, the

[1] Appling *v.* Odum, 46 *Georgia Reports*, 587. See also Sims *v.* Dorsey, 61 *Georgia Reports*, 488.

[2] Almond *v.* Scott & Co., 80 *Georgia Reports*, 95.

title to and right to control and possess the crops grown and raised upon the lands of the landlord by the cropper shall be vested in the landlord until he has received his part of the crops so raised, and is fully paid for all advances made to the cropper in the year said crops were raised to aid in making said crops.[1]

The above recited law and decisions serve to show that the "third and fourth" renter occupies a higher place in the economic scale than does the cropper. The former is, at least in a small way, both manager and capitalist; the latter is, at least in theory, neither manager nor capitalist. The cropping system is a post-bellum product, the "third and fourth" plan of tenancy had its origin in the period before the war.

In view of what has been said heretofore concerning the abundance of land in Georgia in the early decades of the last century, it is needless to say that no great amount of tenancy had arisen before 1860. Inasmuch, however, as most of the lands had come into private ownership at least two decades before the war, it was of course becoming less easy for those without land to find available and desirable tracts. Then too, in some cases, it required energy and daring beyond the amount commonly possessed, for an individual to betake himself and family to a distant piece of land in a frontier section of the state, where he would have to start afresh even to the extent of clearing the land for cultivation and of building a log cabin for shelter. Therefore, those who possessed less than the required amount of aggressiveness remained within the circle of old acquaintances and familiar surroundings, becoming in a few cases, tenants on the poorer parts of the large plantations. They usually agreed in such cases to turn over to the planter one-

[1] *Acts of the General Assembly of Georgia* (1889), p. 113.

third of the grain and one-fourth of the cotton produced on the land thus obtained.[1] It was natural therefore that after the war the system should have been continued and extended in so far as the conditions made such an arrangement possible—that is to say, in so far as the would-be tenant was in position to obtain stock and implements with which to carry on his farming operations, and in so far as the percentages represented the economic importance of the productive factors.

The way is now prepared for an examination of the extent to which the systems of share farming have tended to prevail in the state. Unfortunately, no statistics are available which would indicate the number of farms included in the two categories separately considered. In the United States census reports the two are grouped together as farms operated by share tenants. The best that can be done, therefore, is to get from these figures a view of the prevalence of the two combined and then to interpret and supplement that view in the light of personal observation and enquiry. The following table gives a general view of the wide prevalence of share farming in Georgia.[2]

	1880	*1890*	*1900*
Total number of farms	138,625	171,071	224,266
Number of farms operated by share tenants	43,618	62,181	75,810
Percentage of farms operated by share tenants	31.5	36.4	33.7

[1] The fact that more labor is required in the cultivation of cotton than in the cultivation of corn and other grain accounts for the smaller percentage rent in the case of the former. This means that it takes less labor to produce one hundred units of grain value than to produce one hundred units of cotton value, or, to express the same thing in a different way, more land is required to produce one hundred units of grain value than to produce the same amount of cotton value.

[2] *Abstract of the Twelfth Census*, pp. 294, 295.

The figures show that in 1900 about one-third of the farms of the state were operated by share tenants. In the decade 1880 to 1890 there was not only a large absolute but a relative increase in the number of share farms. In the next decade, however, although there was an increase of about twenty per cent in the absolute number of farms worked on shares, the relative number of farms so operated underwent a seven per cent increase.

This showing suggests the interesting query as to whether or not the year 1890 represents the high-water mark in share farming in Georgia. That is to say, is it likely that the above mentioned relative decrease from 1890 to 1900 is the beginning of a gradual decline of share farming? In attempting to answer this query the two plans of share farming must be considered separately. For, since the two are not so interrelated that they must stand or fall together, it is possible that the relative decrease in the two combined may conceal the fact that one of the systems is increasing, but at a slower rate than the other is decreasing. As a matter of fact the "third and fourth" system attained its widest prevalence in the seventies or early eighties. Since then it has been on the decline so that it now includes only a small percentage of the farms. In answer to enquiries as to why that particular system is no longer widely used, the landlords say that it is an unfair arrangement for them—they can command a larger return through some other system.[1]

[1] An analysis of the way in which pure economic forces have worked out this change will be made in the following chapter. It will there also be pointed out that the same forces are working to overthrow the cropping system, but that the full effect of such forces is delayed in the case of the cropping system because of the operation of a countervailing economic force.

Having seen that the "third and fourth" system is practically a thing of the past, it is in order to see if an analysis of the statistics will throw any light upon the tendencies in the cropping system. A study of the geographical distribution of the farms worked by share tenants for the two dates, 1890 and 1900, reveals a considerable shifting in their prevailing location. In 1890, most of the counties north of a line extending from Columbus to Augusta had a percentage of share farms higher than the average for the state. Another group of counties in the southwestern part of the state also had a high percentage of share tenants. In 1900, this small southwestern group is still found, showing, with slight modifications, a high percentage of share tenants.[1] Aside from this the significant fact is revealed that there has been a northward movement, across about three tiers of counties, of the line which separates the counties showing a percentage of share-worked farms higher than the average for the state from those showing a percentage lower than this average. Most of the middle counties and many of the southwestern counties, that is to say, the main cotton-growing area of the state, suffered a decrease in the relative number of farms operated on shares, while the extreme northern and "pine barren" southern counties suffered an increase in the relative number of farms so worked. In many of the middle counties where in 1890 forty and fifty per cent of the farms were worked by share tenants, in 1900 only fifteen or twenty-five per cent fall into that category. The offset to this relative decrease has been in those sections of the state less inviting economically. This movement taken in connection with other forces yet to be de-

[1] See map in Appendix, *infra*.

scribed[1] seems to warrant the conclusion that the cropping system is already in process of gradual extinction.

Another interesting phase of the matter is the relative number of negroes and whites operating share farms. The *Twelfth Census* is the first to give any information on this subject. According to the returns there given fifty-two per cent of the share farms were operated in 1900 by whites.[2] This showing seems to lead to the conclusion that the negroes are about on a par with the whites in so far as they are ill—or well—affected by the circumstances associated with that system; for the negro share tenants sustain about the same proportion to the white share tenants as the total number of negroes sustains to the total number of whites in the state.

It should be noticed that the section in which the negro share tenants outnumber the white share tenants coincides generally with the cotton belt, which in turn coincides with that section of the state in which the negroes outnumber the whites. It so happens that the section thus marked out is the very district which suffered from 1890 to 1900 a decrease in the relative number of share tenants and is just south of the area within which the share system had its greatest prevalence in 1900. It appears, therefore, that the share system is losing ground in that part of the state where it was supposed to be strongly entrenched, namely, in the negro and cotton belt.

The rapid decay of the "third and fourth" system and the apparent beginning of a relative decline of the cropping system, raise the question as to what tendencies are to be found at work among the other forms of land tenure. Aside from the farms worked by owners there ex-

[1] *Cf.* chapter vi.

[2] *Twelfth Census*, vol. v, p. 69.

ist in the state two other arrangements not differing in essence but unlike in an important particular. In the one, the renter makes an annual cash payment of so much per acre or per farm for the use of the land and improvements thereon. In the other, instead of a money rent, the tenant agrees to pay a definite amount of the produce for the use of the land and improvements.

The money rent is of course the most flexible and most highly wrought of all forms of tenancy. Competition in such cases can the more easily adjust the rent to the varying degrees of soil fertility. The tenant is free to use the land for any crops he may care to grow. The lease may be for one acre or for hundreds of acres; it may be for one year or for a period of years. The tenant is the managing entrepreneur and the capitalist, except in so far as the landlord, through furnishing land, is also capitalist. All risks of crop failure and the like rest in the first instance upon the tenant. As yet this is the least used of all forms of land tenure in Georgia.

Under the other plan, as was said above, the tenant pays the landlord a stipulated *amount* of the product. It differs, therefore, from the share systems, in that, according to the latter arrangements, a definite *part* of the product is turned over to the landlord. In Georgia the plan under consideration is usually called the "standing rent" system and, as indicated above, it has a much wider use than the money rent plan. In the region of its greatest prevalence the rent contract usually calls for a definite amount of cotton. A "one-horse" farm of about thirty acres usually rents for from 1,000 to 1,500 pounds of lint cotton—the amount varying according to the fertility and situation of the land and the price of cotton.[1]

[1] Testimony before the Industrial Commission indicated that the rent is usually from 500 to 1000 pounds of cotton. *Report of the Industrial Commission*, vol. x, p. 46.

In this system the landlord is capitalist directly only to the extent of furnishing the land and appurtenances thereto, while the tenant is for the most part the managing entrepreneur, and capitalist as touching forms of capital other than the land. The important respect in which this differs from the money rental lies in the fact that in the case of the latter the renter assumes all the risk incident to changes in the price of the commodity produced, whereas in the standing rent plan this risk is borne by each in proportion to his respective amount of the product. Another point of difference, but not so important as the one just mentioned, is that the "standing rent" contract calls for the production of a specific commodity, whereas in the case of the money rental the tenant may produce whatsoever he pleases on the land.

In the census reports the "standing rent" and the money rent farms are grouped together as farms operated by cash tenants. It has been indicated in what was said above that a large majority of tenants so classified is composed of "standing rent" tenants—that is, most of the cash tenants pay landlords a stipulated amount of cotton as rent. This fact should be remembered while considering the following figures[1] bearing on the prevalence of cash tenancy:

	1880	*1890*	*1900*
Total number of farms	138,626	171,071	224,266
Number of farms operated by cash tenants	18,557	29,413	58,750
Percentage of farms operated by cash tenants	13.4	17.2	26.2

The first lesson which this table teaches is that there was a marked increase from 1880 to 1900 in the number

[1] *Abstract of Twelfth Census*, pp. 284, 295.

of farms operated by cash tenants. Not alone was the absolute number of farms so worked more than trebled but their relative number was almost doubled—the percentage moved from thirteen to twenty-six. It is significant that the decade 1890 to 1900 showed a larger increase than the preceding decade.

The geographical distribution of the cash tenancies reveals the fact that they have tended to preponderate in the main cotton belt of the state. Although in 1880 the percentage of cash tenants was larger in the counties of the cotton belt than elsewhere, they were then and there outnumbered by the farms worked by share tenants. This was also true in 1890, though the difference was not so great. By 1900, however, the cash tenants had the ascendency in the cotton belt as over against the share tenants—which really means that the "standing renters" outnumbered the "croppers." The belt to which reference is made passes through the middle of the state in a southwesterly direction, taking in as it goes about six tiers of counties and also including most of the counties in the southwestern corner of the state.[1] This is not only the main cotton region of the state but, as will be remembered, it is also the section in which the negroes outnumber the whites.

This suggestion invites a consideration of the relative number of whites and blacks falling within the census category of cash tenants. In 1900 sixty per cent of these tenants were negroes.[2] Throughout the main region where the cash system tends to prevail, the number of negro cash tenants exceeded the number of white cash tenants. Forty-two per cent of the farms of negro farmers were operated by cash tenants; whereas seventeen

[1] See map in Appendix, *infra*. [2] *Twelfth Census*, vol. v, p. 69.

per cent of the farms of white farmers were worked by cash tenants.[1] This seems to be a rather creditable showing for the negroes, but, in order to give a balanced view of the last-mentioned percentages, it should be remembered that the white farms far outnumber the negro farms and fifty per cent of the former are returned as being operated by owners.[2]

In order to make the survey complete a word should be said concerning the farms operated by owners. The census figures[3] on this subject are as follows:

	1880	*1890*	*1900*
Total number of farms	138,626	171,071	224,466
Number of farms operated by owners	76,451	79,477	90,131
Percentage of farms operated by owners	55.1	46.4	40.1

It appears that the ownership operation of farms, although showing an absolute increase of eighteen per cent, has suffered a relative decrease. In 1880, fifty-five per cent of the farms were operated by owners, while in 1900, forty per cent were so operated—a relative decrease of twenty-seven per cent. Upon its surface this seems to be an unfortunate tendency. A little analysis, however, will place the matter in a less unfavorable view.

To say that forty per cent of the farms are operated by owners is not the same as saying that only forty per cent of the owners operate their farms. As was pointed out in another connection the number of landowners possessing up to a few hundred acres of land has been on the increase ever since the civil war. It is safe to say that in so far as these holdings are concerned there has been a considerable increase in the number worked by owners.

[1] *Twelfth Census*, vol. v, p. 69.

[2] *Ibid.*, p. 68.

[3] *Abstract Twelfth Census*, pp. 294, 295.

The larger holdings, however, especially those containing over 500 acres, have been split up into anywhere from five to fifty farms worked by croppers and renters.

More than sixty per cent of the proprietors cultivate their own acres.[1] Most of these, at least in so far as relates to the cotton belt, are relatively small landowners, in whom inhere the combined functions of entrepreneur, capitalist and laborer.

There are other cases of ownership operation of farms in which the landlord is entrepreneur and capitalist, but hires the laborers employed on the farm, sometimes supervising the work in person and sometimes employing a manager for this purpose.[2]

The highest percentages in the number of farms worked by owners are found in the northern and southeastern counties of the state, that is to say, outside the main cotton region in which are large percentages of share- and cash-rented farms.[3] During the decade from 1890 to 1900 the high percentages of ownership-operated farms in the northern and southeastern counties suffered a decrease, and, as will be remembered, during the same period in those two regions there was a noteworthy increase in the number of share farms. It is fair to infer, therefore, that large landowners in those comparatively undeveloped counties are inclined to try the cropping system.

As to the distribution of the ownership-operated farms

[1] This estimate is based upon the fact that there are about 140,000 landowners in Georgia as determined from the tax digests and the further fact that there are 90,000 farms operated by owners as shown in the census.

[2] The merits of this plan in relation to present conditions in Georgia are to be discussed in the closing chapter.

[3] See map in Appendix, *infra*.

between the races, it goes without saying that the whites are to be credited with a very much larger share of them than are the negroes. While most of the negroes who own land also cultivate it in person, and only sixty per cent of the whites who own land cultivate it in person, still the white owners so far outnumber the negro owners that it is useless to try to make an exact statistical comparison of the number of white and negro farms that are operated by owners.

By way of summary it may be said that there are in Georgia six plans of farming based on the relation of the farmer to the soil. Arranged in an ascending order of the economic importance of the farmer in each plan they are as follows:

1. The cropping system in which the cropper is only to a slight extent manager and capitalist. The cropper is for the most part a laborer, and gets one-half of the crop as wages. There are indications that the system has already begun to decline in Georgia.

2. The "third and fourth" system in which the renter is the chief manager and important capitalist, and pays the landlord one-third of the grain and one-fourth of the cotton as rent. This system has been rapidly disappearing, so that now it is found only here and there in the state. The cropping and the "third and fourth" systems constitute, so far as relates to Georgia, what the census calls the share system.

3. The "standing rent" plan in which the tenant is managing entrepreneur and capitalist. Under this plan the tenant pays the landlord a definite amount of the product—usually a fixed number of pounds of cotton. It has shown a great increase during the past decade.

4. The money rental plan represents the highest form of tenancy. In this the tenant is managing entrepreneur

and capitalist. As yet this plan does not have a wide use in the state, though it, too, is on the increase. In this the tenant may or may not be the common laborer; in the plans above mentioned he is usually the main laborer as well as the performer of the specified functions. The "standing rent" and the money rent tenants together make up the census group of cash tenants.

5. Small farms operated by owners. Under this plan all the economic functions center in the owner of the land. It goes without saying that it represents a higher type of farming than any of the preceding. In fact it represents from an ideal point of view the very highest type of farming. It is interesting, therefore, to record the fact that such farming is on the increase in Georgia.

6. The plantation system is placed last, not because it is regarded as the acme of the climax, but because it does give scope for the exercise of a higher order of managing ability than does any of the others. It is farming on a large scale as opposed to farming on a small scale. The landlord is not only the managing entrepreneur to a more important extent than in any of the foregoing cases but he is also a large capitalist and conducts his farming operations through the employment of laborers. This method of farming is on the increase and the next chapter will show that the future is likely to see a considerable extension of the plantation system to take the place of the cropping system.

CHAPTER VI

THE ECONOMIC WORKINGS OF THE SYSTEMS OF LAND TENURE.

IN a fundamental sense there are only two forms of land tenure in Georgia—one is ownership and the other is tenancy. The former, however, as was indicated in the preceding chapter, gives rise to two varieties of farming, while the latter manifests itself in four varieties based on differences in the rent contract. There are, therefore, in the state six varieties of farming based on the relation of the farmer to the soil. It is the purpose of this chapter to analyze the workings of these different land tenure arrangements with special reference to both their efficiency in production and their beneficence in the distribution of the product. The importance of the questions involved makes this chapter the goal of the whole discussion. What has gone before has been presented in order to prepare the way for an intelligent answering of the questions that now arise.

Professor J. B. Clark has drawn a sharp and useful line of distinction between the statics and the dynamics of economic problems.[1] The former has to do with

[1] For a detailed account of what is given here only in broad outline, *cf.* Clark, *The Distribution of Wealth.* It will be evident to those familiar with Professor Clark's contributions to economic theory that the writer is under primary obligation to him for anything of scientific value this chapter may contain. Of course, however, Professor Clark is not to be held responsible for any misapplications, or for any inadequate applications of his theories which the writer may have made.

the fundamental and persistent economic forces; while the latter is concerned with forces of a secondary and fluctuating nature—that is, with the forces of change. In order to appreciate the static forces an ideal condition is assumed in which the economic motive works without let or hindrance and in which the forces of change are absent—there are no changes in the wants of consumers, nor in the amounts of labor and capital used, nor in the methods of employing the two factors. Such a combination of circumstances works so to adjust the labor and capital that all units of each are equally productive and every unit is located where it finds its highest productive efficiency.

The competition which brings about this adjustment in response to the economic motive so operates as to attribute to each factor that part of the product for which it is specifically responsible. The laborer gets as wages the specific product of his labor, while the capitalist gets as interest the specific product of his capital. If one person be at the same time both laborer and capitalist his income is both wages and interest, each determined in the manner just stated. These two categories, wages and interest, exhaust the whole of the static income. The above description precludes the existence of profits in the static realm. Profits are always the result of changes and can exist, therefore, only in a dynamic society.

The static state posits the perfect mobility of labor and capital but presents no movements of these from one group to another for the very good reason that there exist no inducements which could lead to such movements—any change would decrease rather than increase the product per unit as well as the total product. Although the assumptions of the static state present a case very unlike the outward manifestations of real life, as Professor Clark carefully points out, still the conception reveals the nature of the primary and persistent economic forces and presents standard rates both of interest and of wages to which the actual rates tend to conform. When the secondary influences are added to the primary, that is to say, when the forces of change are superimposed upon the fundamental or static forces, a resultant may be obtained conforming to actuality. And more important than all, it is only through a study of static forces that one can understand tendencies, for it is static forces that finally dispose of the effects of dynamic forces.

A lengthy reference has thus been made to one of Professor Clark's contributions to economic theory in order to bring it to bear in the elucidation of the workings of the various systems of land tenure in Georgia. The static workings of economic forces is the foundation upon which the discussion is to proceed. In addition to pointing out the fundamental tendencies it is necessary to a clear understanding of the situation to set forth the dynamic influences which disturb the operations of static law. That such disturbances are at work is evidenced by the fact of changes as outlined in the preceding chapter. If the economic motive worked unhindered and if the six systems persisted without manifesting any relative changes in the number of farms and farmers falling within each category, it would be evident that from the standpoints both of efficiency and of beneficence the systems were on a par. This is true because if any one of the systems possessed points of superiority over the others in either of these respects, there would be a tendency for the farmers to pass over from the inferior to the superior until an equilibrium of advantages would be established.

Again, the fact that there are migrations of labor and capital from one system to another indicates the operation of fundamental static laws, but the slowness of these movements suggests the presence of obstructions in the way of their easy operation. In addition, therefore, to pointing out the alignment of economic forces being wrought out in obedience to static principles, it is desired to indicate the elements of friction which hinder a more rapid realization of the best combination of the forces.

The first element of friction to be considered is the risk[1] incident to farming. Particular reference is now made to the risks involved in efforts directed toward an efficient combination of the productive factors, rather than to the casualties arising out of the uncertain action of physical nature—that is to say, reference is now made to the risks over which man has some control, rather than to those over which he has but slight control. Before beginning a detailed consideration of the former risks, however, a word should be said concerning the manner in which the latter work.

An excess of rain, or a drouth, or some other unfavorable influence of nature may subject the return to a given expenditure of labor and capital to a very considerable curtailment, as compared with the return realized under the action of favorable seasons. It may be said, however, that such risks as these apply to all the farming systems under consideration, and tend, therefore, to exert a deterrent influence upon the flow of labor and capital into the farming industry as a whole, in so far as other, less risky, industries are open to them. This may

[1] For an admirable discussion of the economic nature of risk, *cf.* Willett, *The Economic Theory of Risk and Insurance.*

have important bearings upon the question of land tenure, but it is a phase of the matter not of immediate interest in this connection. It is now desired to point out the varying relations which landlords and tenants sustain to the risks of nature under the several systems of land tenure, and to determine what effect such relations have upon the distribution of the product.

It is found that the share systems entail greater risks upon the landlords than do the cash systems, and *vice versa* for the tenant. According to the share plans the landlord's rent depends upon the size of the crop, whereas under the cash plans the landlord's contract calls for a definite amount of the product or of money regardless of the size of the specific crop. Under the operation of such a dynamic influence as crop contingencies, it is of consequence to know whether the landlord is to have a percentage or an absolute amount of the yield. In the absence of countervailing influences the percentage rent is higher than the absolute rent, because the landlord normally prefers a certainty to an uncertainty, and he accepts the certainty unless an inducement is offered sufficiently large to act as an offset to the disutility due to uncertainty. Of course the same principle operates in the case of the tenant. When he assumes all the risk, as in cash tenancy, he must receive a return somewhat larger to act as an offset to the disutility of uncertainty.

These matters might for theoretical purposes be carried into greater detail, but enough has been said to indicate that in each of the six systems of farming a part of the product may be regarded as compensation for the risks due to natural crop contingencies. This part of the product, therefore, tends to go sometimes to the landlord, sometimes to the tenant, and sometimes to both, according to the system employed. It goes without saying, therefore, that the elimination of this risk would tend to effect changes in the relative number of farms under the several systems. Before passing on to the consideration of other and more important forms of risk, it should be noted that the risk of "crop failure" also exerts an influence in the plan of agricultural credit, tending, of course, to elevate credit prices. These credit prices are so related to other risks also, and to other economic forces that their consideration is deferred a bit.

There are other elements of friction which are in the nature of risks, inasmuch as they too involve uncertainties as to the product of a given combination of labor and capital. The risks above described are due to the irregular action of physical nature and would exist even on the supposition that man's conduct always conformed to the dictates of highly wrought and uniform economic motives. The uncertainties now to be considered are due to the irregular action of economic motives in men and might exist even on the supposition that physical nature's action were uniform from year to year. As a general thing it may be said that the presence of the latter risks really intensifies the action of the former; for if the latter perversions were absent, the risks of nature could be brought within the scope of a pretty definite insurance fund.

It is now proposed to analyze the workings of these more powerful elements of friction. The proper approach to the problem is through the avenue of wants. Just as the satisfaction of wants is the *terminus ad quem* of all economic activity, even so wants are the *terminus ex quo* of all sound economic analysis. Economic activity normally arises in response to economic wants. If the wants be defective in that they are not well balanced with reference to the individual's temporary and abiding well-being, his economic activity is apt to be defective. Among the farmers of Georgia the economic wants vary: as to intensity, from the weakest to the strongest; as to variety, from the simplest to the most complex; as to beneficence, from the lowest to the highest and from the most transient to the most abiding. It goes without saying that not many of the farmers have wants characterized by the highest degree of the qualities just mentioned. This, however, is not so unfortunate as the fact that a very large percentage of them are satisfied with only a modicum of economic goods. This is especially true of the tenants in general and of the "cropping" tenants in particular.

An attempt will now be made to point out the shortcomings of the cropping system because of its inadequate connection with strong economic motives. In the course of the argument the promise made at the beginning of this chapter will be more or less adequately fulfilled, that, namely, of analyzing the workings of the several other plans of farming found to exist in Georgia as well as the cropping system. The reason for emphasizing the workings of the cropping system, and of considering the others only incidentally, will appear as the discussion proceeds.

It will be remembered that the cropping arrangement arose out of an anomalous situation. Its original purpose was to meet the needs of those without capital, and so to relate those thus circumstanced to the crop as to overcome their erratic disposition. Under this plan the landlord nominally exercises control over the industry. In practice, however, and for reasons that will be given, the landlord does not exercise that degree of direct supervision necessary for successful results. This leaves the management in the precarious hands of those not capacitated to bring about the most effective co-operation of the productive factors. The croppers do not as a rule make plans with reference to the future, and bend their energies toward the realization of those plans. They are content if they can make some arrangement whereby they may be enabled to get the bare necessaries of life throughout the year that immediately concerns them.[1]

It is in the midst of such a situation that the credit system works its rigorous part. No doubt a conscious mental alertness on the part of these croppers would cast off the burden of the credit system in less than a half-dozen years. But it is useless to speculate upon what these croppers might accomplish in the way of extricating themselves from their unfortunate predicament by using economy, foresight, perseverence and other elements of a superior psychological organization which they do not possess. Since science is primarily concerned with things as they are, it is sufficient here to indicate that the absence of the above-mentioned qualities not only lessens the well-being of the workers immediately concerned, but also entails an extra cost upon society as a whole.

So long as these risks continue, and so long as the cropping system, of which they are a part, is employed, it is likely that the credit system will continue to weigh heavily upon the croppers. But the situation does not call for any fantastic measures of relief, for, as was pointed out in the last chapter, the cropping system has already begun to show a relative decline, and, before this chapter is finished, it will be shown that in the presence of funda-

[1] For further consideration of the inadequate connection of the cropping system with economic motives see below, p. 105.

mental static law the system is doomed to utter extinction.

Reference has already been made to the fact that these credit percentages are being transferred from the merchants to the landlords, as the latter are becoming able to discount the accounts of their tenants at the stores of the merchants.[1] The conditions which are making this possible have also been adverted to. In so far as the landlord's improved condition is due to the higher prices received for cotton during the past five or six years, the cropper's situation has also improved. Since he receives one-half of the cotton raised the higher prices have been a boon to him. These forces have contributed to lessen the risks connected with making advances of supplies to farmers so that the situation seems to warrant the statement made by many supply merchants to the effect that there are now less discrepancies than formerly between the credit and cash prices of goods. To the extent that this is true, the lot of the cropper is now more tolerable than in the past.

It is now in order to inquire why fundamental static law working in a dynamic society will ultimately discard the cropping system as it exists in Georgia to-day. There are several reasons, each leading to the same general conclusion, namely, that a larger return is obtainable from some other combination of the productive forces.

In the first place, the cropping plan is not elastic enough for a dynamic society. Owing to the increase of population, land is becoming more and more important as a factor in production—a fact which posits a presumption against the permanency of a fixed percentage plan of distribution in agriculture. The working of the prin-

[1] *Supra*, p. 59.

ciple involved is admirably illustrated in the case of the "third and fourth" system. In the preceding chapter[1] it was pointed out that this particular system had been practically abandoned in Georgia and the reason there ascribed for its decay is that the landlords say they regard it as an unfair arrangement for themselves. The landlord's reason is thoroughly sound and legitimate; nevertheless, when it is remembered that the system had a wide prevalence twenty-five years ago, it is well worth while to subject the matter to a little closer analysis.

At the time of its origin and development the "third and fourth" system was based upon a sound economic principle, namely, the imputing to the land of that fraction of the product for which it is economically responsible. Land was relatively abundant in those days; but as the population of the state has increased, land has become a more and more important economic factor, so that the part of the product imputable to the land is no longer represented by the percentages of former days. The failure of the system to give scope for the operation of a fundamental economic principle has practically effected its overthrow. It is only in a non-progressive community that such a fixed percentage plan of distribution in agriculture can be a permanent arrangement.

If the above is a correct explanation of the decay of the "third and fourth" system, why has not the same force operated to overthrow the cropping system, inasmuch as it, too, is based upon an inflexible imputation principle? It had its origin in a period of relative land abundance, just as was true of the "third and fourth" system, yet it has continued to increase in importance certainly up to within a decade of the present time.

[1] *Supra*, p. 84.

The explanation of this apparent contradiction is to be found in the fact that, in the cropping system, the landlord supplies not only land, but the other forms of capital as well. While from the static standpoint land and other forms of capital yield the same income per unit, nevertheless, in a dynamic view of the same matter two opposite tendencies are to be seen superimposed upon the fundamental static fact. On the one hand, it is the tendency for land rent to rise per superficial unit; on the other hand, it is the tendency for interest on other forms of capital to fall. So the landlord in the cropping system through the operation of these counterbalancing dynamic forces has been enabled to realize a return commensurate with the economic importance of the productive factors which he has supplied.

It is natural, therefore, that the "third and fourth" system should have disappeared earlier and more rapidly than the cropping system. It is not surprising, however, to find that the latter has already begun to show evidences of decline. But it would be surprising if the cropping system should not continue gradually to disappear, even aside from the influence of certain forces, yet to be considered, which are tending to give considerable impetus to the movement away from the system. So much for the first count against the cropping system.

In the second place, the fact that land is becoming scarcer in relation to population means that greater wisdom must be brought to bear in its utilization than has heretofore been necessary. In view of the characteristics which were given above as inhering in the average cropper, it is safe to say that not much land improvement is likely to come through his initiative. Even on the supposition that he possesses ability and is inclined to make improvements, the fact that he possesses no permanency of tenure would suggest to him the possibility of his failing to reap the benefits which even the share system would give him from such improvements.

This leads to the third count against the system, namely, that it supplies no adequate incentive to either the landlord or the cropper to do more than is called for by the customary terms of the contract. If either of them does anything extra, that is to say, if the landlord furnishes more and better capital goods, or if the cropper takes extra pains in the cultivation of the crop, or himself furnishes extra capital goods, the return expected from such additional expenditures must be twice as large as is necessary to compensate for the additional outlay. This is true, unless there is a co-ordinating head for the business, so that as a balance against the extra capital furnished by the landlord, an adequate amount of extra labor could be required from the cropper. But in case efficient management is called to this task it would not long be content with the limitations of the share system—it would devise another system, and it is already doing this very thing in Georgia.[1]

[1] One instance of the way in which the difficulty under consideration was disposed of in the case of the cropping system may be given. Personal inquiries have been made as to the historical reason for the cropper's paying for one-half of the commercial fertilizers used in making the crop—this being the only form of capital goods he helps to furnish. The answers that have been received are inadequate. The following explanation is ventured: Immediately after the war, when the cropping system arose, commercial fertilizers were not used at all. Then the landlord furnished the entire stock of capital goods used in making the crop while the cropper supplied only the labor. Experimentation later demonstrated that fertilizers increased the yield very considerably. According to the landlord's reckoning, one-half of the increased return due to the use of fertilizers was not large enough to offset the cost of the stuff. Inasmuch as the cropper was to share equally in the increased return, it was thought proper for him to bear one-half the extra expense. It was, perhaps, unconsciously assumed that the landlord's

The situation is about as follows: The future is sure to demand the use of improved methods of production. The landlord will not be willing to add more and better machinery to his farm unless he either personally directs the use of such improvements or employs some one to do this managing work for him. When he increases the capital invested in the industry and assumes the management so as to lessen the risks and bring about the most efficient combination of the labor and the capital he will not be content with a plan of distribution that gives him only one-half of the gains. That is not the way the economic motive normally works, nor is it the way it is likely to work in Georgia.

So far as the farming industry alone is concerned there are three main avenues leading away from the cropping system, and each of them is offering substantial inducements to those connected with the system to migrate into another. One avenue leads the cropper to the direct acquisition of a small farm for himself. To the extent that he displays energy and foresight enough to acquire such a proprietorship it is likely that he possesses ability enough to manage his farming operations prudently, and he therefore makes an important addition to the state's citizenry. Some have already taken this route away from the cropping system, some are doing so now, and some will do so in the years that are to come. There are no indications, however, that this avenue is to be

security for the advance of fertilizers by the merchants was an offset to the cropper's extra work in "putting in" the guano.

It may be said, too, that some of the landlords now have the croppers pay for one-half of the cotton seed planted. This is an illustration of the plans that must be adopted when operating under rigid imputation principles. But there are limits to these schemes, and a progressive society soon passes beyond these limits and must discard the system beset with such limitations.

used to any considerable extent by the croppers. They are going to leave the cropping system, and ultimately many of them, or of their descendants, will become independent landowning farmers ; but the route they are to take is not so direct as that indicated by avenue number one.

The second avenue open to croppers leads them into tenancy proper. This means the payment, as rent, not of a fixed percentage of the product, but of a stated amount either of product or of money, which can be made to vary according to the specific economic importance of particular pieces of land. Tenancy proper tends to center responsibility and risks upon the tenant. He, therefore, can reap, in the first instance, the benefits of good management and skill in agriculture. Of course, this does not mean that the tenant could continue to appropriate all the extra gains due to his efficient allignment of the productive factors. Land would tend to get its due part, but the actual rent might lag somewhat behind the static rent if unusually progressive methods were employed by the tenant, thus making it possible for him to realize considerable entrepreneur's profits. The point which it is desired to emphasize is that the tenant system proper is not inherently bad. It is not only elastic enough to tend to give the tenant the entire part of the product imputable to his labor, but it is also a system in which it is possible for all the profits to inure to the benefit of the tenant, thus offering him the highest inducements to adopt the most efficient methods of production.

It goes without saying that those who have managed well under this system may soon pass into the ownership of land. It is not so evident, however, that it is easy for the croppers to pass over into tenancy. It is to be inferred from what is said above concerning the lack of thrift characteristic of the croppers, that it would mean neither progress for the farmers in general nor improvement for the croppers in particular, for them to become immediately independent tenants. Of course it is desirable that they should become tenants, but only in so far as they are capable of managing farms efficiently. A few of these croppers might now become tenants with advantage to themselves and the general farming interests. The selective process, however, has carried over, and continues to carry over into the tenant class most of those qualified to do justice to their opportunity. Some have, no doubt, passed over without possessing proper qualifications and are to be otherwise disposed of in the adjustments that are taking place. It is of interest to recall the fact brought out in the preceding chapter[1] that recent years have shown an encouragingly large increase in the number of cash tenants.

Since neither the first nor the second avenue is to furnish the way through which large percentages of the croppers are to pass from the cropping system to something better, there remains to be pointed out the road through which most of them are destined to be led by reason of the operation of pure economic law.

The impulse which is giving rise to the movement is acting from above downward—that is to say, the large landowner, rather than the cropper, is the initiator of the change that will redound to the benefit of both. The large landowners will oust the croppers as croppers but retain them in another relation. The motive that is to cause the abandonment of the cropping system is a desire on the part of the landlords to bring about the most efficient organization of the productive forces at their

[1] *Supra*, p. 88.

command. The plan to which reference is made may be called the plantation system because it bears a certain analogy to the system that existed under that name before the war. The old plantation was worked by slave labor, the new plantation is worked by free labor. It is the plan of farming on a large scale to which the production of cotton is admirably adapted. It is the plan of hiring laborers, putting them under efficient management, and conducting the operations of farming in accordance with approved business methods.

It is a well-known fact that most of the croppers, especially those of them who are negroes, make splendid farmers when put under the direction of one who knows how to manage. The cropping system does not offer sufficient inducements for landlords to undertake either in person or through a hired manager this much-needed work of supervision. The plantation system offers the highest inducement for efficient management.

The specific gains for the landlord are entrepreneur's profits and the increased productiveness of land and other capital goods. It has been demonstrated in hundreds of cases in recent years that, by intelligent supervision and co-ordination of the forces, farming can be made to yield in Georgia a large profit over and above the outlay in wages and interest.

As an example of the capabilities of the system under discussion the case of a large planter in Coweta county is given. Near his home there is a small tract of land consisting of about thirty acres, the greater portion of which fifteen years ago was considered worn out and worthless. In the early nineties he began to give personal direction to the work of this farm—using hired labor exclusively. The result was that for the year 1895, when, owing to the low price of cotton, many of the farmers were unable to meet their current accounts, this man realized above expenses from this small piece of land over $400 including the rent of the land, or over $300 after a liberal rent allowance is made. And this result was obtained without the annual expenditure for improvements of more capital than is shown below. The expense and income accounts for this farm, according to his books, were as follows:

OUTLAY.

One hand—$12.50 per month	$150.00	
Extra labor—chopping, *etc.*	64.11	
Picking 37,304 lbs. cotton at 30 cents per 100	111.10	
Total outlay for labor		$325.21
Implements—hoes, plows, *etc.*		7.85
Fertilizers		126.10
Blacksmithing		4.00
Ginning		29.90
Bagging and ties		25.00
Mule rent		25.00
Mule feed		75.00
		$618.06

INCOME.

12,521 lbs. cotton at .07½	$939.82	
750 bu. cotton seed at .12½	93.75	
		1,033.57
		$415.51

Supposing the rent of the land and the interest and sinking fund on other capital goods not specified should amount to $115 there is still left as wages of superintendence and net profits $300. This amount of course would hardly be an adequate reward for superintendence, much less would it include any profit, if it had taken the entire time of the landlord to look after so small a farm as one of thirty acres. As a matter of fact this was as play for that planter and it would take a farm twenty times as large to engage his full powers.[1]

[1] In fact, this planter owns a farm about one hundred times as larg

Assuming that an exceptional case has been cited, as it certainly is, and assuming that the planter who brought about such results possesses unusual managing ability, as he most assuredly does, still the results are worthy of a close examination and comparison with the results normally obtained under the cropping system.[1]

As a usual thing a cropper and his family working one mule produce from five to eight bales of cotton together with perhaps fifty or seventy-five dollars' worth of corn and other produce. It is on the basis of a liberal estimate therefore to assume that his crop turns out about as follows:

8 bales of cotton, 4000 lbs., at .08 per pound	$320.00
210 bu. cotton seed at .15	36.00
60 bu. corn at .60	36.00
	$392.00

From this amount the following common expenses are to be deducted:

3 tons fertilizers	$60.00
Ginning 8 bales of cotton	10.00
Bagging and ties	8.00
	$78.00

This leaves $314 to be divided between the landlord

as the patch above referred to and some twenty-five or thirty families are cultivating it. In view of his other interests he employs a manager to supervise his large farming operations. The planter devoted only odd moments to the 30-acre patch, except that when he had a large body of extra laborers employed in it as in the case of "hoeing over" the crop, he would remain with the hands in the field. In such cases he would personally supervise the work of about twenty hands, and so definite were his methods, that if a hand should wantonly stop work five or ten minutes before the working day was over, his wages for that day suffered by just so much.

[1] It is to be understood that the case has been given in *illustration* of the reasoning in this chapter and not in its *support*.

and the cropper, making the share of each $157. In the end the cropper gets whatever is left over after his family account is settled at the neighboring merchant's. From the landlord's $157 the following items of expense are to be deducted:

Mule rent	$20
Mule feed	50
Interest and sinking fund on tools	15
	$85

This leaves to the credit of the landlord a balance of $72—a fund out of which is to come an offset against the risks assumed, a fund out of which is to come the wages for whatever measure of superintendence he may have exercised, a fund out of which is to come the rent on thirty acres of land! It is not surprising that during the period of declining prices in the cotton markets thousands of farmers became bankrupt. It is not surprising that the more alert of the large landowners are beginning to turn away from a system so uneconomic in its workings and are turning to the plantation-wages system which has in store large gains for the enterprising owner of many acres.

It is now in order to see what effect the change is likely to have on the economic condition of the cropper who becomes in name, as well as in fact, a wage earner upon the plantation. To many it will appear that the cropper is taking a step backward rather than a step forward. Over against such a view, the opinion is ventured that the plantation-wages system will not only add much to the efficiency of the erstwhile cropper but that it will also operate beneficently upon him as compared with the cropping system. This opinion is based upon several considerations.

As a point of departure in the argument it may be

said that the total product will be larger, giving rise to a considerable element of profit. This will lead to strong competition among the planters, with the result that labor will tend to get larger wages per unit. This is true notwithstanding the fact that the relative amount of the product going to the laborer under the plantation system may be smaller than in the case of the cropping system. It is of more importance to the laborer, however, that he should get a larger absolute amount although a smaller percentage, rather than a smaller absolute amount even though it may be a larger percentage of the total. The same fundamental economic law works in the two cases—the laborer tends to get that part of the product for which he is economically responsible. The fact is, he is economically responsible for a larger absolute amount under the plantation system than under the cropping system and fundamental economic law will tend to give this larger amount to him.

Figures may be used to illustrate what has been said concerning the advantages accruing to the laborer under the plantation-wages system as over against the cropping system. The cropper's net share rarely amounts to over $150. In the case given above his share was $157. As an indication that this is a liberal calculation it may be said that merchants usually make $100 the limit of the line of credit obtainable by a one-mule cropper. Under the wages plan cited above the laborer got as wages $150 and in addition thereto a house to live in just as in the cropping system. If these were all the facts to be considered it appears that the greater independence enjoyed under the cropping plan might offset the slight shade of economic advantage on the side of the wages plan. There are, however, two important additional considerations which overwhelmingly carry the argument in favor of the plantation-wages system in so far as relates to the economic well-being of the laborer.

In the first place, in addition to the $125 or $150 earned by the head of the family, whose labor under the plantation-wages system will be needed throughout the twelve months of the year, there are to be added the earnings of the other members of the family during special seasons of the year. For instance, in the case of the wages farm described above, $64 were paid for extra labor in cultivating the crop, such as chopping and hoeing, and $111 were paid for extra labor employed in "picking" the cotton. It thus appears that $175 were paid in wages in addition to the $150 paid the regular laborer. A large percentage of this extra pay would normally go into the pockets of the regular laborer's family. Granting that the extra wages vary with the size of the crop, and granting also that the normal plantation yield will be for many years far below a bale of cotton per acre, as was almost the case in the example farm, still the important fact remains that the system promises the laborer a larger family income than the cropping system gives.

In the second place, the laborer will be out from under the yoke of the credit system. At the present time the cropper can get only a little more than $80 worth of goods with his $100, or only about $100 worth of goods with the $120 he receives under the cropping system. Under the wages plan the laborer can buy for cash and can therefore get one dollar's worth of goods for each of his dollars. Even supposing the laborer got absolutely the same money income in the plantation system as in the cropping system the elimination of the credit evil would of itself justify the laborer in welcoming the change.

There has been much complaint on account of the scarcity of farm labor in Georgia within recent years. There are two leading causes for this migration of laborers from the farm. One is the recent rapid development of the cotton-manufacturing industry in the state. This has given rise to a large stream of white labor from the farms into the factories. In all probability most of these factory laborers have come from the class of tenants and croppers. They have gone to the factories and placed themselves under the control of efficient managers because they could make more under the factory wages system than in self-directed farming. The other stream has been that of black labor moving into the towns and cities, sometimes in answer to an economic motive, sometimes in obedience to social instincts and sometimes in response to a combination of the two stimuli. The two motives meet in the case of many of the wages employments into which they have entered. For instance, this is true of the mining industry of Alabama, which has carried away from Georgia, especially from the western counties, many of the negro tenants and croppers. The plantation-wages system will tend to reverse this stream, or at least to counteract the tendency of negroes to leave the farms. For, in addition to the economic inducements which it will offer, it is also calculated to respond more adequately to the negro's social instincts than does the cropping system. The croppers are usually isolated on the plantation, and do not work together In the plantation-wages system the work is conducted for the most part in groups under supervision.

Finally, it should be noted that the plantation-wages system subjects the laborer to an industrial training of great educational value. All who think know that it is worse than folly to attempt to give any people an education without an economic substratum. The industrial training which the negroes received in slavery is a matter of great significance in the development of that race. They need yet more industrial training and such training as progressive plantation farming is well suited to supply. The need is hardly less urgent in the case of the white croppers.

Thus far the changes have been considered in their relation to the economic well-being of those immediately concerned in the terms of distribution. It is true, considerable emphasis was laid upon the efficiency of the plan of plantation production; but this was done without referring in particular to the ultimate social effects of this efficiency. In ultimate analysis it means a race in social service. The profits that will arise will induce more and more farmers, in so far as they are capacitated, to adopt the efficient organization of their forces. This means in the long run cheaper cotton, and cheaper cotton is a great social desideratum.

This suggests the query as to what effect such a working out of static law will have on the small proprietors, who, let it be hoped, will continue to increase in number. Owing to the elements of economic friction which hinder the rapid realization of static demands, the process that has been outlined will work itself out very slowly. Those who are unable to compete in the production of cotton will, therefore, have plenty of time in which to adjust themselves to the production of those crops out of which they can realize most. What they will produce—whether it is to be cotton or something else or cotton and many things else—it is not now and here necessary to say.

APPENDIX

APPENDIX

TABLE A

WHITE AND NEGRO OWNERSHIP OF LAND IN GEORGIA BY COUNTIES FOR THE YEAR 1903, COMPILED FROM THE COUNTY TAX DIGESTS FOR THAT YEAR

1903	White Owners			Negro Owners			Total Owners		
Counties	Number...	Acres ...	Average size....	Number...	Acres ...	Average size....	Number...	Acres ...	Average size....
Appling	1160	371126	319.9	199	20726	104.1	1359	391852	288
Baker	406	202939	499.8	69	11804	171.0	475	214743	452
Baldwin	548	139568	254.6	163	9808	50.1	711	149376	210
Banks....	771	120281	156.0	41	3173	77.4	812	123454	164
Bartow	1270	251915	198.3	137	5825	42.5	1407	257740	183
Berrien	1600	498385	311.4	86	4247	49.1	1686	502632	298
Bibb	951	143318	150.7	310	4458	14.3	1261	147776	117
Brooks	950	276496	291.0	253	17742	70.1	1203	294238	244
Bryan	486	176799	364.1	149	7899	53.0	635	184698	290
Bulloch	1614	457924	283.7	195	15035	77.0	1809	472959	261
Burke	1072	558000	520.5	214	33705	110.7	1286	591705	460
Butts	690	112392	162.8	41	1458	35.5	731	114850	198
Calhoun	339	163056	481.0	54	7209	133.7	393	170265	433
Camden	325	15586	47.9	631	9409	14.9	956	24995	26
Campbell	782	126306	161.5	39	1909	48.9	821	128215	156
Carroll	2215	289008	130.4	71	5553	78.2	2286	294561	128
Catoosa	663	91596	138.1	13	649	50.0	676	92245	136
Charlton	396	143829	363.4	42	4689	111.6	438	148518	339
Chatham...........	629	174475	277.3	497	6239	12.5	1126	180614	160
Chattahoochee	340	144672	425.5	58	7112	122.6	398	151784	380
Chattooga...........	794	157653	198.5	46	3247	70.5	840	160900	191
Cherokee	1388	240699	174.1	36	2980	87.2	1424	243679	171
Clarke	448	66180	147.7	235	5353	22.7	683	71533	104
Clay	355	126789	356.8	56	11638	207.8	411	138427	336
Clayton.............	763	91083	119.3	17	1253	73.7	780	92333	118
Clinch	591	298277	504.7	64	5168	80.7	655	303445	463
Cobb	1783	205163	115.0	77	6897	89.5	1860	202060	114
Coffee	1102	516829	468.9	192	30146	157.0	1294	546975	422
Colquitt	1172	268826	229.3	23	536	23.3	1195	269362	225
Columbia	578	174655	302.1	155	9621	68.5	733	184276	251
Coweta	1152	266951	231.7	108	5781	53.5	1260	272732	216

1903	White Owners			Negro Owners			Total Owners		
Counties	Number..	Acres ...	Average size....	Number..	Acres ...	Average size....	Number..	Acres ...	Average size....
Crawford	653	191992	294.0	112	13157	117.4	765	205149	268
Dade	535	106975	199.9	20	455	22.7	555	106430	191
Dawson	673	123539	183.5	4	470	117.5	677	124009	183
Decatur	1824	590772	323.8	647	50930	77.1	2471	641702	259
De Kalb	1728	160212	92.7	86	2100	24.4	1814	181212	99
Dodge	1124	230664	205.2	255	19776	77.5	1379	250440	181
Dooly	1432	363388	252.9	145	14203	97.9	1577	377591	239
Dougherty	312	174755	560.1	209	13573	64.9	521	188328	361
Douglas	841	114193	135.7	61	4968	81.4	902	119161	132
Early	735	285787	388.8	193	19689	102.0	928	305476	329
Echols	277	122138	440.9	7	2255	322.1	284	124393	438
Effingham	882	229110	248.4	338	11829	35.0	1220	240939	197
Elbert	991	204792	206.6	80	9052	113.1	1071	213844	199
Emanuel	1408	378030	268.4	224	21293	95.0	1632	399323	244
Fannin	1338	236467	176.7	4	165	41.2	1342	236632	176
Fayette	765	116931	152.8	21	1341	63.8	786	118272	150
Floyd	1397	264635	189.6	204	12043	59.0	1601	276678	172
Forsyth	1060	152520	143.8	35	2223	63.5	1095	154743	141
Franklin	1254	190412	151.8	44	2978	67.6	1298	193390	148
Fulton	1803	90885	50.4	123	1153	9.3	1926	92038	47
Gilmer	1377	252968	183.7	4	527	131.7	1381	253495	183
Glascock	392	84372	215.2	10	541	54.1	402	84913	211
Glynn	212	53834	253.9	541	14918	27.5	753	68752	91
Gordon	1279	209696	163.9	41	2233	54.5	1320	211929	160
Greene	729	235312	322.7	131	7761	59.2	860	243073	283
Gwinnett	1961	285720	145.7	68	2551	37.5	2029	288271	142
Habersham	1420	208860	141.3	93	2956	31.7	1513	211816	140
Hall	1580	242236	151.3	56	3972	70.9	1636	246108	150
Hancock	811	257055	316.9	272	21467	78.9	1083	278522	257
Haralson	1339	152001	113.5	58	3292	56.7	1397	155293	111
Harris	951	261411	274.8	163	17209	105.5	1114	278620	250
Hart	998	145573	145.8	55	3410	62.0	1053	148983	141
Heard	920	180433	196.1	75	7238	96.5	995	187671	188
Henry	1050	189455	180.4	85	3639	42.8	1135	193194	170
Houston	838	325515	388.4	153	16860	110.2	991	342375	345
Irwin	1740	398926	229.2	120	13475	112.2	1860	412401	221
Jackson	1555	233935	150.4	98	5841	59.6	1653	239776	145
Jasper	877	219396	250.1	125	9827	78.6	1002	229223	228
Jefferson	961	312902	325.6	141	10364	73.5	1102	323266	293
Johnson	723	156241	216.1	33	2695	81.6	756	158936	210
Jones	613	214402	349.9	113	14915	132.0	726	229317	315
Laurens	1441	417290	289.5	287	23904	83.2	1728	441194	256
Lee	340	200962	591.0	181	17420	96.2	521	228382	438
Liberty	861	307351	356.9	1134	48675	42.9	1995	356026	178
Lincoln	635	152994	240.9	34	3777	111.1	669	156771	234

1093	White Owners			Negro Owners			Total Owners		
Counties	Number..	Acres ...	Average size....	Number..	Acres ...	Average size....	Number..	Acres ...	Average size....
Lowndes	955	297203	311.2	382	24031	62.9	1337	321234	240
Lumpkin	910	184833	203.1	31	1745	56.2	941	186588	198
Macon	675	210464	311.7	94	7241	77.0	769	217705	283
Madison	875	164550	188.0	62	3428	55.2	937	167978	179
Marion	667	212023	317.8	53	7254	136.8	720	219277	305
McDuffie	512	151493	295.8	60	5348	89.1	572	156841	274
McIntosh	237	55728	235.1	692	13854	20.0	929	69582	74
Meriwether	1205	280485	232.7	81	5604	69.1	1286	286089	222
Miller	465	126761	272.6	62	5967	96.2	527	132728	251
Milton	686	86545	126.1	9	304	33.7	695	86849	125
Mitchell	955	300215	314.3	144	22249	154.5	1099	322464	293
Monroe	1117	278618	249.4	272	15770	57.9	1389	294388	211
Montgomery	1313	390518	297.4	249	16737	67.2	1562	407255	260
Morgan	712	211336	296.8	119	7079	59.4	831	218415	262
Murray	848	174416	205.6	5	140	28.0	853	174556	204
Muscogee	774	126928	163.9	374	6288	16.8	1148	133216	116
Newton	834	158612	190.1	126	5790	45.8	960	164402	171
Oconee	665	110409	166.0	62	4034	65.0	727	114443	157
Oglethorpe	838	258274	308.2	70	10958	156.4	908	269232	296
Paulding	1308	178808	136.7	56	4099	73.1	1364	182907	134
Pickens	805	149089	185.2	6	618	103.0	811	149707	184
Pierce	866	272673	314.8	138	6559	47.5	1004	178232	277
Pike	1068	185359	173.5	81	3731	46.0	1149	189090	164
Polk	860	166096	193.1	196	10771	54.9	1056	176867	167
Pulaski	867	250215	288.5	173	16129	93.2	1040	266344	256
Putnam	527	204926	388.8	52	6906	132.8	579	211832	365
Quitman	219	96161	439.0	21	3263	155.3	240	99424	414
Rabun	891	190052	213.3	10	912	91.2	901	190964	211
Randolph	703	252194	358.7	79	10331	130.7	782	262525	335
Richmond	919	179343	195.1	124	4245	34.2	1043	183588	176
Rockdale	579	78653	135.8	35	3115	88.9	614	81768	133
Schley	334	98743	295.6	28	5207	186.0	362	104050	287
Screven	1273	380815	299.1	263	17691	67.2	1536	398506	259
Spalding	712	113134	158.8	151	4634	30.7	863	117768	136
Stewart	645	274929	426.2	96	14591	152.0	741	289520	390
Sumter	779	286636	369.7	197	14360	72.8	976	300996	308
Talbot	745	215245	288.9	114	9273	81.3	859	224518	261
Taliaferro	433	108488	250.5	108	8808	81.5	541	117296	216
Tattnall[1]	1652	486397	288.3	266	18970	71.3	1918	505367	263
Taylor	749	213586	285.1	114	8470	74.2	863	222056	257
Telfair	710	140302	197.6	228	12202	53.5	938	152504	162
Terrell	670	195348	291.5	122	12101	99.1	792	207449	261
Thomas	1619	412708	254.9	502	29529	58.8	2111	442237	209
Towns	549	92546	168.5	3	310	103.3	552	92857	168

[1] 1902 Digest used instead of 1903.

1903	White Owners			Negro Owners			Total Owners		
Counties	Number..	Acres ...	Average size....	Number..	Acres ...	Average size....	Number..	Acres ...	Average size....
Troup.....	880	255486	290.3	126	9162	72.7	1006	264468	263
Twiggs....	609	194332	319.1	83	9980	120.2	692	204312	295
Union	1110	184460	166.1	7	156	22.2	1117	184616	165
Upson.....	744	164625	221.2	71	9766	137.5	815	174391	213
Walker ...	1557	229691	147.5	75	3005	40.0	1632	232696	142
Walton ...	1223	224576	183.6	73	6174	84.5	1296	230750	178
Ware	696	191316	274.8	100	5480	54.8	796	196796	247
Warren....	580	173580	299.2	69	2182	31.6	649	175762	270
Washingt'n[1]	1190	395287	332.1	107	11205	104.7	1297	406492	313
Wayne	1071	285793	266.8	159	10377	65.2	1230	296170	240
Webster ...	388	123294	317.7	53	6332	119.4	441	129626	294
White	640	140105	218.9	18	1167	64.2	658	141272	214
Whitfield ..	1125	116011	103.1	44	2330	52.9	1169	118341	101
Wilcox	1070	255631	238.9	76	12431	163.5	1146	268062	233
Wilkes[1] ...	861	282114	327.6	153	14232	93.0	1014	296346	292
Wilkinson .	871	267524	307.1	79	8239	104.2	950	275763	290
Worth[1]....	1351	386228	285.8	151	12202	80.8	1502	398430	265
Total....	124647	29769720	238.8	18708	1246455	66.6	143355	31016175	216.3

[1] 1902 Digest used instead of 1903.

TABLE B

LAND PROPRIETORSHIPS OF WHITES IN 31 TYPICAL COUNTIES OF GEORGIA CLASSIFIED BY ACREAGE FOR THE YEARS 1873, 1880, 1890 AND 1902, COMPILED FROM THE TAX RETURNS FOR THOSE YEARS

WHITE PROPRIETORSHIPS

1873

Counties	Under 3 acres	3 to 10	10 to 20	20 to 50	50 to 100	100 to 175	175 to 260	260 to 500	500 to 1000	1000 acres and over	Acres	No. of Proprietorships	Average size
Banks[1]	2	4	6	20	81	159	99	119	52	12	134439	554	242
Berrien	2	1	4	14	47	82	118	181	93	51	286381	593	482
Burke[1]	2	5	4	14	46	122	104	167	162	136	537920	762	706
Butts	0	1	3	7	68	134	116	84	39	10	113365	462	245
Camden	0	2	5	12	18	35	26	39	23	24	85762	184	466
Campbell	0	2	4	14	111	185	116	101	36	6	125814	575	218
Catoosa	1	0	1	14	87	143	51	70	30	8	96520	405	238
Clay	0	1	0	6	17	66	77	65	43	26	120508	302	400
Coweta	2	7	7	21	121	229	171	149	87	54	267012	848	314
Decatur	1	1	1	15	71	150	264	129	211	113	572705	956	599
Dougherty	0	4	2	1	14	13	26	12	54	65	182304	191	954
Forsyth[1]	1	11	3	154	197	260	110	131	24	5	141874	896	158
Gilmer	0	4	1	36	134	382	83	172	45	7	188731	864	218
Greene	0	12	7	22	43	104	67	149	87	54	242818	545	445
Houston	0	1	1	10	42	92	136	130	133	101	342381	646	530
Jasper	3	6	1	17	49	125	120	125	98	42	226009	586	385
Johnson	0	0	0	3	19	63	55	70	51	25	147402	286	515
Liberty	0	0	2	7	30	86	81	113	119	92	323849	530	611
Lincoln	0	1	3	10	25	45	47	66	56	45	154953	298	520
Lowndes	0	2	0	7	11	61	104	159	85	69	295757	498	593
Madison	2	4	3	17	54	153	101	126	61	21	162167	542	299
Newton	3	11	6	35	86	189	125	102	61	20	166302	638	260
Paulding	0	2	2	223	270	272	127	94	21	3	143665	1014	141
Polk[1]	4	3	4	73	62	125	59	90	38	18	134518	476	282
Putnam	1	4	3	1	26	61	55	89	83	62	220214	385	572
Sumter	10	6	6	6	62	115	149	134	98	58	280398	644	435
Talbot	0	0	3	4	33	98	89	125	100	42	219048	494	443
Telfair	0	0	1	1	4	20	78	57	44	21	104836	226	464
Troup	1	2	6	21	54	200	132	163	112	45	255763	735	348
Union	1	1	3	25	93	215	77	117	52	14	166611	598	278
Wilkes[1]	1	1	5	7	31	85	90	109	105	88	294374	523	562
Total	37	99	97	817	2006	4069	3053	3437	2303	1337	6734398	17255	388.6

[1] 1874 Digest used. The one for 1873 was not available.

WHITE PROPRIETORSHIPS

1880

Counties	Under 3 acres	3 to 10	10 to 20	20 to 50	50 to 100	100 to 175	175 to 260	260 to 500	500 to 1000	1000 acres and over	Acres	No. of Proprietorships	Average size
Banks	4	3	5	35	143	175	101	119	46	9	133860	640	209
Berrien	2	3	8	28	79	142	162	230	112	79	425648	845	503
Burke	0	10	4	34	84	178	151	172	162	141	539004	936	575
Butts	3	9	9	26	123	153	102	92	31	11	114063	559	204
Camden [1]	1	8	5	13	24	34	34	45	32	31	122142	227	538
Campbell	2	8	5	32	137	209	116	83	42	8	127232	642	198
Catoosa	2	4	3	34	113	170	48	77	24	6	96369	481	199
Clay	0	2	4	11	37	84	77	53	45	28	127426	341	373
Coweta	2	7	8	32	167	249	155	166	90	44	267367	920	291
Decatur	1	6	7	36	138	248	323	158	213	111	536403	1241	432
Dougherty	1	3	0	3	13	11	32	19	48	63	187021	193	969
Forsyth	10	15	10	166	249	275	120	113	24	2	150617	984	153
Gilmer	1	3	5	74	210	421	125	156	56	14	237099	1065	223
Greene	3	12	3	34	91	134	97	165	100	39	244428	678	360
Houston	0	3	6	13	55	120	118	168	112	86	330048	681	484
Jasper	8	10	5	26	79	157	120	138	95	39	220753	677	326
Johnson	0	0	1	23	43	136	103	90	60	27	153552	483	318
Liberty	1	7	9	27	58	109	106	146	126	93	389409	682	571
Lincoln	1	4	2	13	33	64	62	79	55	43	156523	356	439
Lowndes	9	5	5	20	49	122	144	175	99	65	312842	693	451
Madison	5	3	12	28	112	183	119	123	44	22	164807	651	253
Newton	5	7	15	60	151	205	119	103	48	16	160148	729	220
Paulding	26	7	4	305	299	298	135	110	24	5	170376	1213	140
Polk	4	8	6	108	125	145	89	84	47	15	143086	631	226
Putnam	2	4	5	8	46	84	90	84	91	54	199777	468	426
Sumter	14	18	17	13	79	139	178	135	101	54	285374	748	381
Talbot	0	0	6	16	52	128	130	137	82	42	212285	593	358
Telfair	0	1	2	12	18	51	122	61	38	14	95785	319	300
Troup	2	4	6	26	75	145	132	156	111	49	262468	706	371
Union	2	0	6	55	133	252	82	119	56	18	181408	723	251
Wilkes	0	5	4	20	69	103	105	129	113	72	289216	620	467
Total	111	179	187	1331	3084	4924	3597	3685	2327	1300	7036536	20725	339.5

[1] 1879 Digest used.

WHITE PROPRIETORSHIPS

1890

Counties	Under 3 acres	3 to 10	10 to 20	20 to 50	50 to 100	100 to 175	175 to 260	260 to 500	500 to 1000	1000 acres and over	Acres	No. of Proprietorships	Average size
Banks	8	10	9	54	185	206	113	99	36	6	127983	726	176
Berrien	5	12	17	88	163	234	205	233	124	80	488475	1161	420
Burke	4	4	11	37	113	223	169	192	184	141	579045	1078	537
Butts	8	12	8	47	149	167	106	78	36	7	111609	618	180
Camden	9	77	78	53	9	7	1	1	2	4	17052	241	70
Campbell	7	9	14	46	161	209	100	74	46	11	130126	677	192
Catoosa	6	12	8	59	116	189	67	69	21	3	96159	550	175
Clay	1	3	6	19	44	78	65	53	52	25	111453	346	322

WHITE PROPRIETORSHIPS

1890—*Concluded*

COUNTIES	Under 3 acres	3 to 10	10 to 20	20 to 50	50 to 100	100 to 175	175 to 260	260 to 500	500 to 1000	1000 acres and over	Acres	No. of Proprietorships	Average size
Coweta	7	8	23	56	189	276	175	163	89	38	267275	1024	261
Decatur	15	16	14	92	238	345	337	202	158	98	524461	1515	346
Dougherty	24	9	5	5	14	16	36	20	51	60	184086	240	767
Forsyth	5	7	12	186	273	311	115	119	25	3	151770	1056	143
Gilmer	3	3	7	97	257	460	156	168	47	14	238682	1212	196
Greene	3	6	7	36	95	175	112	146	83	48	232432	711	327
Houston	5	3	2	23	94	163	148	147	127	81	339333	793	427
Jasper	10	16	10	52	114	209	137	142	82	34	218212	807	270
Johnson	3	4	5	39	102	198	129	104	53	19	172284	656	262
Liberty	8	12	18	52	108	133	114	131	119	85	366295	780	469
Lincoln	2	1	3	16	57	104	77	81	53	28	147451	422	349
Lowndes	19	10	11	26	53	201	140	197	115	47	294420	819	359
Madison	6	7	15	59	196	213	106	121	36	21	166253	780	213
Newton	6	15	18	88	204	245	112	110	53	10	166550	861	193
Paulding	13	7	8	263	356	314	163	106	30	5	173463	1265	137
Polk	22	9	12	131	144	165	112	99	54	12	157178	760	206
Putnam	3	7	4	16	61	117	91	98	79	52	213989	528	405
Sumter	14	15	15	19	90	181	125	153	98	51	285532	761	380
Talbot	0	2	6	24	73	143	145	144	86	44	232041	667	347
Telfair	1	5	8	17	59	94	159	102	43	19	135875	507	268
Troup	0	3	5	32	98	207	131	147	107	48	257415	778	330
Union	3	6	11	110	231	296	126	146	39	20	196342	988	198
Wilkes	3	7	6	20	106	173	117	137	103	59	283265	731	386
Total	223	317	376	1862	4152	6052	3889	3782	2231	1173	7066506	24058	293.7

WHITE PROPRIETORSHIPS

1902

COUNTIES	Under 3 acres	3 to 10	10 to 20	20 to 50	50 to 100	100 to 175	175 to 260	260 to 500	500 to 1000	1000 acres and over	Acres	No. of Proprietorships	Average size
Banks	5	12	17	81	218	203	109	89	29	4	126684	767	165
Berrien	23	26	51	155	271	382	228	247	136	81	545597	1600	341
Burke	3	13	12	53	117	191	154	192	198	137	557231	1070	520
Butts	16	14	15	73	165	200	91	81	33	6	113026	694	162
Camden	11	72	95	90	17	21	6	9	3	4	18703	328	57
Campbell	21	14	20	87	192	202	94	105	32	8	127105	775	164
Catoosa	15	24	35	127	160	173	60	65	19	3	93023	681	136
Clay	2	2	4	18	40	83	70	67	41	26	119917	353	339
Coweta	17	15	27	88	227	295	188	160	84	37	264739	1138	232
Decatur	6	29	25	152	391	418	309	217	134	83	569374	1764	322
Dougherty	92	9	10	5	11	22	40	12	49	54	185137	304	627
Forsyth	5	8	13	164	280	309	118	111	18	3	151990	1029	147
Gilmer	4	10	22	143	318	459	174	163	42	11	246689	1346	183
Greene	2	11	11	56	117	187	126	136	74	46	237573	766	309
Houston	0	7	10	42	115	201	139	159	120	68	329370	861	382
Jasper	7	7	10	71	159	224	153	154	63	34	218632	882	247
Johnson	3	6	8	65	137	238	141	107	50	15	167478	770	217
Liberty	8	27	30	95	142	175	115	129	82	61	267993	864	309

WHITE PROPRIETORSHIPS

1902—*Concluded*

COUNTIES	Under 3 acres	3 to 10	10 to 20	20 to 50	50 to 100	100 to 175	175 to 260	260 to 500	500 to 1000	1000 acres and over	Acres	No. of Proprietorships	Average size
Lincoln	4	6	8	41	111	150	115	103	55	21	154169	614	251
Lowndes	13	28	21	61	107	242	133	187	86	49	298048	927	321
Madison	10	16	12	104	270	226	105	109	40	20	165244	912	181
Newton	13	13	17	87	195	226	104	92	50	13	157049	810	194
Paulding	11	8	13	267	360	340	157	107	23	6	174254	1292	134
Polk	15	15	14	165	190	220	101	102	50	12	170056	884	192
Putnam	6	3	3	22	69	129	79	103	69	51	199347	534	373
Sumter	4	10	12	38	102	166	140	153	92	52	287319	769	373
Talbot	3	6	7	29	70	168	160	155	88	29	218382	715	305
Telfair	4	5	14	55	117	160	191	87	49	8	146114	690	212
Troup	2	6	8	37	136	214	160	157	106	31	251925	857	294
Union	5	10	19	128	299	322	126	130	37	14	194298	1090	178
Wilkes	8	12	12	45	148	210	141	152	92	51	282114	871	323
Total	338	444	575	2644	5251	6754	4027	3840	2044	1038	7138586	26957	264.8

TABLE C

LAND PROPRIETORSHIPS OF NEGROES IN 31 TYPICAL COUNTIES OF GEORGIA, CLASSIFIED BY ACREAGE FOR THE YEARS 1873, 1880, 1890 AND 1902, COMPILED FROM THE TAX RETURNS FOR THOSE YEARS

NEGRO PROPRIETORSHIPS

1873

COUNTIES	Under 3 acres	3 to 10	10 to 20	20 to 50	50 to 100	100 to 175	175 to 260	260 to 500	500 to 1000	1000 acres and over	Acres	No. of Proprietorships	Average size
Banks [1]	0	0	0	3	2	3	1	0	0	0	866	9	96
Berrien	0	0	0	0	0	2	3	1	0	0	1538	6	256
Burke [1]	1	4	3	5	15	9	11	5	3	0	7771	56	138
Butts	0	0	0	0	0	0	0	0	0	0	0	0	0
Camden	0	1	4	12	16	15	2	2	1	0	4999	53	94
Campbell	0	0	0	0	2	4	0	2	0	0	1173	8	146
Catoosa	0	0	0	0	1	3	0	0	0	0	540	4	135
Clay	0	0	0	2	1	4	2	0	0	0	1120	9	124
Coweta	0	0	0	3	5	5	2	0	0	0	1500	15	100
Decatur	1	0	2	2	8	17	25	5	0	0	10751	60	179
Dougherty	0	0	0	0	1	2	1	0	0	0	500	4	125
Forsyth [1]	0	0	0	14	6	2	1	0	0	0	1476	23	64
Gilmer	0	0	0	0	1	2	2	0	0	0	880	5	176
Greene	0	0	0	3	4	11	2	1	0	0	2595	21	123
Houston	0	0	0	1	2	5	4	0	0	0	1784	12	148
Jasper	1	0	1	2	2	1	0	1	0	0	627	8	78
Johnson	0	0	0	0	0	1	0	0	0	0	100	1	100
Liberty	0	0	2	1	1	1	0	0	1	0	739	6	123
Lincoln	0	0	0	0	1	6	0	0	0	0	730	7	104
Lowndes	0	0	0	0	0	1	9	5	0	0	4453	15	297
Madison	0	0	0	1	3	5	1	1	0	0	1371	11	124
Newton	0	3	1	5	9	1	1	0	0	0	1126	20	56
Paulding	0	0	0	17	2	4	0	0	0	0	1206	23	52
Polk [1]	2	0	2	10	3	7	2	1	0	0	2228	27	82
Putnam	0	0	0	0	0	1	1	2	1	0	1791	5	358
Sumter	2	1	2	2	8	9	2	0	0	0	2109	26	81
Talbot	0	0	0	1	3	1	1	0	0	0	540	6	90
Telfair	0	0	0	0	1	1	2	1	0	0	1057	5	211
Troup	0	3	0	3	5	1	1	1	0	0	1037	14	81
Union	0	0	0	0	0	0	0	0	0	0	0	0	0
Wilkes [1]	11	27	2	1	5	6	2	1	0	0	1952	55	35
Total	18	39	19	88	107	130	78	29	6	0	58556	514	113.9

[1] 1874 Digest used. The one for 1873 was not available.

NEGRO PROPRIETORSHIPS

1880

COUNTIES	Under 3 acres	3 to 10	10 to 20	20 to 50	50 to 100	100 to 175	175 to 260	260 to 500	500 to 1000	1000 acres and over	Acres	No. of Proprietorships	Average size
Banks	0	0	0	5	12	7	3	1	0	0	2665	28	95
Berrien	0	0	0	4	3	1	1	1	1	0	1549	11	140
Burke	0	1	2	7	23	21	21	14	4	0	17461	93	187
Butts	0	2	0	0	0	2	0	0	0	0	208	4	52
Camden [1]	5	24	41	74	53	20	8	5	0	0	11844	230	51
Campbell	2	0	1	8	9	5	1	3	0	0	2744	29	94
Catoosa	1	0	0	1	0	2	0	0	0	0	352	4	88
Clay	5	4	1	1	4	7	7	0	0	0	2553	29	81
Coweta	5	3	2	9	11	6	4	0	0	0	2559	40	63
Decatur	5	2	2	17	35	66	50	11	2	0	28586	190	150
Dougherty	0	1	1	0	4	2	1	0	3	0	2506	12	208
Forsyth	3	1	4	19	9	7	1	0	0	0	2604	44	59
Gilmer	0	0	0	1	7	6	2	0	0	0	1895	16	118
Greene	1	8	7	18	10	8	3	0	1	0	3574	56	63
Houston	1	3	3	4	20	20	7	4	1	0	7384	63	117
Jasper	1	8	4	3	10	4	5	2	0	0	2970	37	80
Johnson	0	0	0	2	6	4	0	1	0	0	1273	13	98
Liberty	3	20	53	145	111	35	14	8	2	1	24322	392	61
Lincoln	0	0	0	0	2	3	0	0	0	0	605	5	121
Lowndes	12	14	10	12	10	11	10	6	3	0	10456	88	118
Madison	0	0	1	4	15	12	2	0	0	0	2888	34	84
Newton	9	5	5	6	23	9	2	1	0	0	3866	60	64
Paulding	0	0	1	17	8	4	1	0	0	0	1950	31	62
Polk	1	3	2	31	15	9	3	1	0	0	4331	65	66
Putnam	3	2	0	0	2	5	4	4	0	1	3975	21	189
Sumter	31	18	5	14	8	15	8	3	0	0	5940	102	58
Talbot	2	0	1	3	11	9	7	1	0	0	3664	34	107
Telfair	0	3	1	14	8	7	9	1	0	0	3731	43	86
Troup	10	9	5	6	10	4	4	1	0	0	2541	49	52
Union	0	0	0	0	0	0	0	0	0	0	0	0	0
Wilkes	0	0	2	9	12	16	2	1	0	0	3944	42	93
Total	100	131	154	434	451	327	180	69	17	2	174940	1865	93.8

[1] 1879 Digest used.

NEGRO PROPRIETORSHIPS

1890

COUNTIES	Under 3 acres	3 to 10	10 to 20	20 to 50	50 to 100	100 to 175	175 to 260	260 to 500	500 to 1000	1000 acres and over	Acres	No. of Proprietorships	Average size
Banks	0	2	2	6	9	9	4	2	0	0	3443	34	101
Berrien	3	10	7	10	7	9	4	1	1	0	3690	52	71
Burke	7	6	6	21	32	32	24	19	6	1	23834	154	155
Butts	20	4	3	3	6	2	1	0	0	0	980	39	25
Camden	72	245	79	12	0	0	0	0	0	0	2500	408	61
Campbell	0	1	0	8	11	5	1	1	0	0	1909	27	74
Catoosa	0	0	1	2	3	0	0	0	0	0	324	6	54
Clay	4	9	3	2	4	19	8	0	1	0	4663	50	93

NEGRO PROPRIETORSHIPS

1899—*Concluded*

COUNTIES	Under 3 acres	3 to 10	10 to 20	20 to 50	50 to 100	100 to 175	175 to 260	260 to 500	500 to 1000	1000 acres and over	Acres	No. of Proprietorships	Average size
Coweta	7	3	6	5	19	10	6	3	0	0	4660	59	79
Decatur	30	27	40	58	71	65	54	18	9	0	39129	372	105
Dougherty	4	3	1	4	2	7	14	4	4	1	9238	44	211
Forsyth	2	4	0	16	9	2	3	0	0	0	2294	36	63
Gilmer	0	0	1	0	1	2	1	0	0	0	565	5	113
Greene	4	7	7	23	13	15	3	1	1	0	5671	84	67
Houston	3	10	8	20	22	24	10	9	2	1	13313	109	122
Jasper	27	19	5	11	22	14	2	3	1	0	5389	104	51
Johnson	0	1	2	9	10	9	6	2	0	0	4226	39	108
Liberty	37	64	96	256	176	58	19	14	4	1	41227	725	56
Lincoln	0	0	0	0	4	4	2	2	0	0	1914	12	159
Lowndes	43	49	39	50	35	23	15	11	3	1	16113	269	59
Madison	1	5	4	9	20	8	1	1	0	0	3200	49	66
Newton	19	11	3	12	22	10	2	0	2	0	4035	81	49
Paulding	2	0	1	20	12	5	1	0	0	0	2403	41	58
Polk	23	5	9	43	15	10	4	0	0	0	5093	109	46
Putnam	3	3	3	2	12	6	8	8	1	0	7021	46	153
Sumter	38	39	16	15	22	20	15	8	2	0	12304	175	70
Talbot	9	15	6	9	36	17	14	1	0	0	8070	107	75
Telfair	2	12	11	24	20	16	10	2	0	0	6745	97	69
Troup	10	14	9	14	20	22	6	4	1	0	7884	100	78
Union	0	2	1	4	2	1	0	0	0	0	431	10	43
Wilkes	1	9	3	10	17	20	4	2	1	0	7111	67	106
Total	371	579	372	678	664	444	242	116	39	5	249469	3510	71.0

NEGRO PROPRIETORSHIPS

1902

COUNTIES	Under 3 acres	3 to 10	10 to 20	20 to 50	50 to 100	100 to 175	175 to 260	260 to 500	500 to 1000	1000 acres and over	Acres	No. of Proprietorships	Average size
Banks	2	1	3	7	16	7	3	0	0	0	2979	39	76
Berrien	43	18	12	20	15	9	3	2	0	0	4392	122	35
Burke	6	12	5	20	40	44	37	42	11	1	32262	218	148
Butts	11	9	3	5	7	4	2	0	0	0	1556	41	38
Camden	47	191	188	145	19	4	1	0	0	0	8372	595	13
Campbell	3	0	4	19	13	6	0	0	0	0	2190	45	48
Catoosa	1	1	1	7	3	1	0	0	0	0	503	14	36
Clay	7	7	3	3	8	15	12	7	4	1	11510	67	172
Coweta	36	8	11	7	12	15	5	5	0	0	5372	99	54
Decatur	63	79	65	120	128	89	41	18	7	1	45788	611	74
Dougherty	130	2	2	4	6	11	11	3	4	2	10205	175	58
Forsyth	1	3	1	14	8	3	4	0	0	0	2298	34	67
Gilmer	0	0	1	1	1	1	1	0	0	0	510	5	102
Greene	5	8	8	24	27	22	6	3	0	0	7524	103	73
Houston	1	10	27	23	39	28	17	10	5	0	16837	160	105
Jasper	24	19	8	21	21	14	6	4	3	1	9512	121	78
Johnson	0	5	6	4	12	12	1	1	0	0	2994	41	73
Liberty	89	183	205	305	218	74	26	14	3	0	53060	1117	47

NEGRO PROPRIETORSHIPS

1902—*Concluded*

COUNTIES	Under 3 acres....	3 to 10........	10 to 20	20 to 50	50 to 100	100 to 175	175 to 260........	260 to 500	500 to 1000	1000 acres and over........	Acres	No. of Proprietorships....	Average size.....
Lincoln	0	0	1	2	9	9	5	3	0	0	3780	29	131
Lowndes	73	58	54	67	44	43	20	13	4	0	26312	376	69
Madison	7	9	10	9	18	7	1	1	0	0	2982	62	48
Newton	22	10	8	18	21	11	6	1	0	0	5171	97	53
Paulding	2	1	0	18	15	15	0	1	0	0	3611	52	69
Polk	24	12	11	92	31	19	8	2	1	0	11063	200	55
Putnam	4	4	3	5	9	11	5	2	1	0	7589	44	172
Sumter	41	36	14	16	22	25	16	11	4	0	13958	185	75
Talbot	11	8	6	11	39	28	10	2	0	1	10280	116	88
Telfair	7	21	35	48	33	31	10	2	0	0	10536	187	56
Troup	9	17	11	10	21	31	4	4	1	0	8659	108	80
Union	1	2	0	5	0	0	0	0	0	0	169	8	21
Wilkes	20	26	7	18	28	30	15	2	2	2	14232	150	95
Total	690	760	713	1068	883	619	276	153	50	9	336216	5221	64.3

TABLE D

LAND PROPRIETORSHIPS OF BOTH WHITES AND NEGROES IN 31 TYPICAL COUNTIES OF GEORGIA, CLASSIFIED BY ACREAGE FOR THE YEARS 1873, 1880, 1890 AND 1902, COMPILED FROM THE TAX RETURNS FOR THOSE YEARS

WHITE AND NEGRO PROPRIETORSHIPS

1873

COUNTIES	Under 3 acres	3 to 10	10 to 20	20 to 50	50 to 100	100 to 175	175 to 260	260 to 500	500 to 1000	1000 acres and over	Acres	No. of Proprietorships	Average size
Banks [1]	2	4	6	23	83	162	100	119	52	12	135205	563	240
Berrien	2	1	4	14	47	84	121	182	93	51	287929	599	480
Burke [1]	3	9	7	19	61	131	115	172	165	136	545691	818	667
Butts	0	1	3	7	68	134	116	84	39	10	113365	462	245
Camden	0	3	9	24	34	40	28	41	24	24	90761	237	383
Campbell	0	2	4	14	113	189	116	103	36	6	126987	583	217
Catoosa	1	0	1	14	88	146	51	70	30	8	97060	409	237
Clay	0	1	0	8	18	70	79	65	43	26	121628	310	392
Coweta	2	7	7	24	126	234	173	149	87	54	268512	863	311
Decatur	2	1	3	17	79	167	289	134	211	113	583456	1016	574
Dougherty	0	4	2	1	15	15	27	12	54	65	182803	195	937
Forsyth [1]	1	11	3	168	203	262	111	131	24	5	143350	919	156
Gilmer	0	4	1	36	135	384	85	172	45	7	189611	869	218
Greene	0	12	7	25	47	115	69	150	87	54	245413	566	433
Houston	0	1	1	11	44	97	140	130	133	101	344165	658	523
Jasper	4	6	2	19	51	126	120	126	98	42	226636	594	381
Johnson	0	0	0	3	19	64	55	70	51	25	147502	287	514
Liberty	0	0	4	8	31	87	81	113	120	92	324588	536	605
Lincoln	0	1	3	10	26	51	47	66	56	45	155683	305	510
Lowndes	0	2	0	7	11	62	113	164	85	69	300210	513	585
Madison	2	4	3	18	57	158	102	127	61	21	163538	553	295
Newton	3	14	7	40	95	190	126	102	61	20	167428	658	254
Paulding	0	2	2	240	272	276	127	94	21	3	144871	1037	139
Polk [1]	6	3	6	83	65	132	61	91	38	18	136746	503	271
Putnam	1	4	3	1	26	62	56	91	84	62	222005	390	571
Sumter	12	7	8	8	70	124	151	134	98	58	282507	670	422
Talbot	0	0	3	5	36	99	90	125	100	42	219588	500	439
Telfair	0	0	1	1	5	21	80	58	44	21	105893	231	458
Troup	1	5	6	24	59	201	133	164	112	45	256800	749	342
Union	1	1	3	25	93	215	77	117	52	14	166611	598	278
Wilkes [1]	12	28	7	8	36	91	92	110	105	88	296326	578	512
Total	55	138	116	905	2113	4199	3131	3466	2309	1337	6792954	17769	382.2

[1] 1874 Digest used. The one for 1873 was not available.

WHITE AND NEGRO PROPRIETORSHIPS

1880

Counties	Under 3 acres	3 to 10	10 to 20	20 to 50	50 to 100	100 to 175	175 to 260	260 to 500	500 to 1000	1000 acres and over	Acres	No. of Proprietorships	Average size
Banks	4	3	5	40	155	182	104	120	46	9	136525	668	204
Berrien	2	3	8	32	82	143	163	231	113	79	427197	856	499
Burke	0	11	6	41	107	199	172	186	166	141	556465	1029	540
Butts	3	11	9	26	123	155	102	92	31	11	114271	563	203
Camden [1]	6	32	46	87	77	54	42	50	32	31	133986	457	293
Campbell	4	8	6	40	146	214	117	86	42	8	129976	671	193
Catoosa	3	4	3	35	113	172	48	77	24	6	96721	485	199
Clay	5	6	5	12	41	91	84	53	45	28	129979	370	351
Coweta	7	10	10	41	178	255	159	166	90	44	269926	960	281
Decatur	6	8	9	53	173	314	373	169	215	111	564989	1431	394
Dougherty	1	4	1	3	17	13	33	19	51	63	189527	205	924
Forsyth	13	16	14	185	258	282	121	113	24	2	152511	1028	148
Gilmer	1	3	5	75	217	427	127	156	56	14	238994	1081	221
Greene	4	20	10	52	101	142	100	165	101	39	248002	734	338
Houston	1	6	9	17	75	140	125	172	113	86	337432	744	453
Jasper	9	18	9	29	89	161	125	140	95	39	223723	714	313
Johnson	0	0	1	25	49	140	103	91	60	27	154825	506	306
Liberty	4	27	62	172	169	144	120	154	128	94	413731	1074	385
Lincoln	1	4	2	13	35	67	62	79	55	43	157128	361	435
Lowndes	21	19	15	32	59	133	154	181	102	65	323298	781	413
Madison	5	3	13	32	127	195	121	123	44	22	167695	685	244
Newton	14	12	20	66	174	214	121	104	48	16	163974	789	207
Paulding	26	7	5	322	307	302	136	110	24	5	172326	1244	138
Polk	5	11	8	139	140	154	92	85	47	15	147417	696	211
Putnam	5	6	5	8	48	89	94	88	91	55	203752	489	416
Sumter	45	36	22	27	87	154	186	138	101	54	291314	850	343
Talbot	2	0	7	19	63	137	137	138	82	42	215949	627	344
Telfair	0	4	3	26	26	58	131	62	38	14	99516	302	275
Troup	12	13	11	32	85	149	136	157	111	49	265009	755	351
Union	2	0	6	55	133	252	82	119	56	18	181408	723	251
Wilkes	0	5	6	29	81	119	107	130	113	72	293160	662	442
Total	211	310	341	1765	3535	5251	3777	3754	2344	1302	7211476	22590	319.2

[1] 1879 Digest used. The one for 1880 was not available.

WHITE AND NEGRO PROPRIETORSHIPS

1890

Counties	Under 3 acres	3 to 10	10 to 20	20 to 50	50 to 100	100 to 175	175 to 260	260 to 500	500 to 1000	1000 acres and over	Acres	No. of Proprietorships	Average size
Banks	8	12	11	53	194	215	117	101	36	6	131426	760	173
Berrien	8	22	24	98	170	243	209	234	125	80	492165	1213	405
Burke	11	10	17	58	145	255	193	211	190	142	602879	1232	489
Butts	28	16	11	50	155	169	107	78	36	7	112589	657	171
Camden	81	322	157	65	9	7	1	1	2	4	19552	649	30
Campbell	7	10	14	54	172	214	101	75	46	11	132125	704	187
Catoosa	6	12	9	61	119	180	67	69	21	3	96473	556	173
Clay	5	12	9	21	48	97	73	53	53	25	116116	396	293

WHITE AND NEGRO PROPRIETORSHIPS

1890—*Concluded*

COUNTIES	Under 3 acres	3 to 10	10 to 20	20 to 50	50 to 100	100 to 175	175 to 260	260 to 500	500 to 1000	1000 acres and over	Acres	No. of Proprietorships	Average size
Coweta	14	11	29	61	208	286	181	166	89	38	271935	1083	251
Decatur	45	43	54	150	309	410	391	220	167	98	563590	1887	298
Dougherty	28	12	6	9	16	23	50	24	55	61	193324	284	680
Forsyth	7	11	12	202	282	313	118	119	25	3	154064	1092	141
Gilmer	3	3	8	97	258	462	157	168	47	14	239247	1217	197
Greene	7	13	14	59	118	190	115	147	84	48	238103	795	299
Houston	8	13	10	43	116	187	158	156	129	82	352646	902	391
Jasper	37	35	15	63	136	223	139	145	83	34	223601	910	246
Johnson	3	5	7	48	112	207	135	106	53	19	176510	695	254
Liberty	45	76	114	308	284	191	133	145	123	86	407522	1505	270
Lincoln	2	1	3	16	61	108	79	83	53	28	149365	434	344
Lowndes	62	59	50	76	88	224	155	208	118	48	310533	1088	285
Madison	7	12	19	68	216	221	107	122	36	21	169453	829	204
Newton	25	36	21	100	226	255	114	110	55	10	170585	942	181
Paulding	15	7	9	283	368	319	164	106	30	5	175866	1306	132
Polk	45	14	21	174	159	175	116	99	54	12	162271	869	186
Putnam	6	10	7	18	73	123	99	106	80	52	221010	574	315
Sumter	52	54	31	34	112	201	140	161	100	51	297836	926	321
Talbot	9	17	12	33	109	160	159	145	86	44	240111	774	310
Telfair	3	17	19	41	79	110	169	104	43	19	142620	604	236
Troup	10	17	14	46	118	229	137	151	108	48	265299	878	302
Union	3	8	12	114	233	297	126	146	39	20	196773	990	198
Wilkes	4	16	9	30	123	193	121	139	104	59	290376	800	362
Total	594	896	748	2440	4816	6496	4131	3898	2270	1178	7315975	27568	265.3

WHITE AND NEGRO PROPRIETORSHIPS

1902

COUNTIES	Under 3 acres	3 to 10	10 to 20	20 to 50	50 to 100	100 to 175	175 to 260	260 to 500	500 to 1000	1000 acres and over	Acres	No. of Proprietorships	Average size
Banks	7	13	20	88	234	210	112	89	29	4	129663	806	160
Berrien	66	44	63	175	266	391	231	249	136	81	549989	1722	319
Burke	9	25	17	73	157	235	191	234	209	138	589494	1288	457
Butts	27	23	18	78	172	204	93	81	33	6	114592	735	155
Camden	58	263	283	235	36	25	7	9	3	4	27075	923	29
Campbell	24	14	24	106	205	208	94	105	32	8	129295	820	169
Catoosa	16	25	36	134	163	174	60	65	19	3	93526	695	134
Clay	9	9	7	21	48	98	82	74	45	27	131427	420	312
Coweta	53	23	38	95	239	310	193	165	84	37	270111	1237	218
Decatur	69	108	90	272	519	507	350	235	141	84	615162	2375	216
Dougherty	222	11	12	9	17	33	51	15	53	56	195342	479	407
Forsyth	6	11	14	178	288	312	122	111	18	3	154288	1063	145
Gilmer	4	10	23	144	319	460	175	163	42	11	247199	1351	182
Greene	7	19	19	80	144	209	132	139	74	46	245097	869	282
Houston	1	17	37	65	154	229	156	169	125	68	346207	1021	339
Jasper	31	26	18	92	180	238	159	158	66	35	228144	1003	227
Johnson	3	11	14	60	149	250	142	108	50	15	170472	811	209
Liberty	97	210	235	400	360	249	141	143	85	61	321053	1981	162

WHITE AND NEGRO PROPRIETORSHIPS

1902—*Concluded*

COUNTIES	Under 3 acres	3 to 10	10 to 20	20 to 50	50 to 100	100 to 175	175 to 260	260 to 500	500 to 1000	1000 acres and over	Acres	No. of Proprietorships	Average size
Lincoln	4	6	9	43	120	159	120	106	55	21	157949	643	245
Lowndes	86	86	75	128	151	285	153	200	90	49	324360	1303	248
Madison	17	25	22	113	288	233	106	110	40	20	168226	974	172
Newton	35	23	25	105	216	237	110	93	50	13	162220	907	178
Paulding	13	9	13	285	375	355	157	108	23	6	177865	1344	132
Polk	39	27	25	257	221	239	109	104	51	12	181119	1084	167
Putnam	10	7	6	27	78	140	84	105	70	51	206936	578	358
Sumter	45	46	26	54	124	191	156	164	96	52	301277	954	315
Talbot	14	14	13	40	109	196	170	157	88	30	228662	831	275
Telfair	11	26	49	103	150	191	201	89	49	8	156650	877	178
Troup	11	23	19	47	157	245	164	161	107	31	260584	965	269
Union	6	12	19	133	299	322	126	130	37	14	194467	1098	177
Wilkes	28	38	19	63	176	240	156	154	94	53	296346	1021	290
Total	1028	1204	1288	3712	6134	7373	4303	3993	2094	1047	7474802	32178	232.2

MAPS

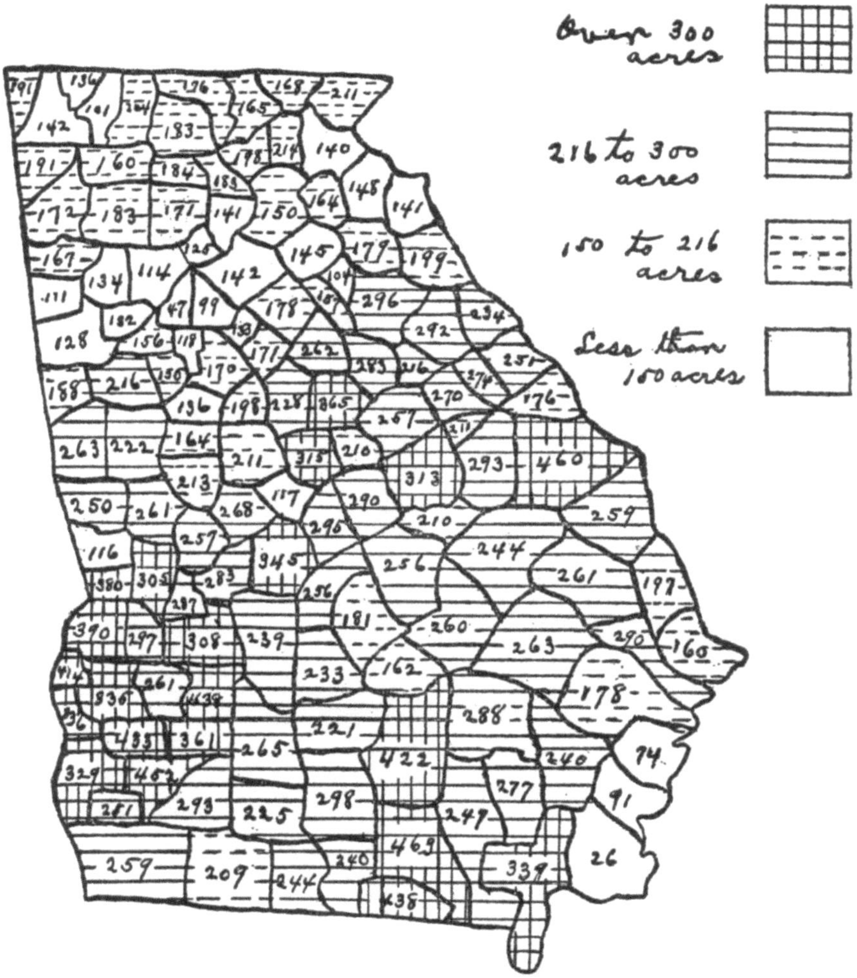

AVERAGE SIZE OF PROPRIETORSHIPS IN GEORGIA BY COUNTIES IN 1903. AVERAGE FOR THE STATE IS 216 ACRES. See pp. 41–43 of the text.

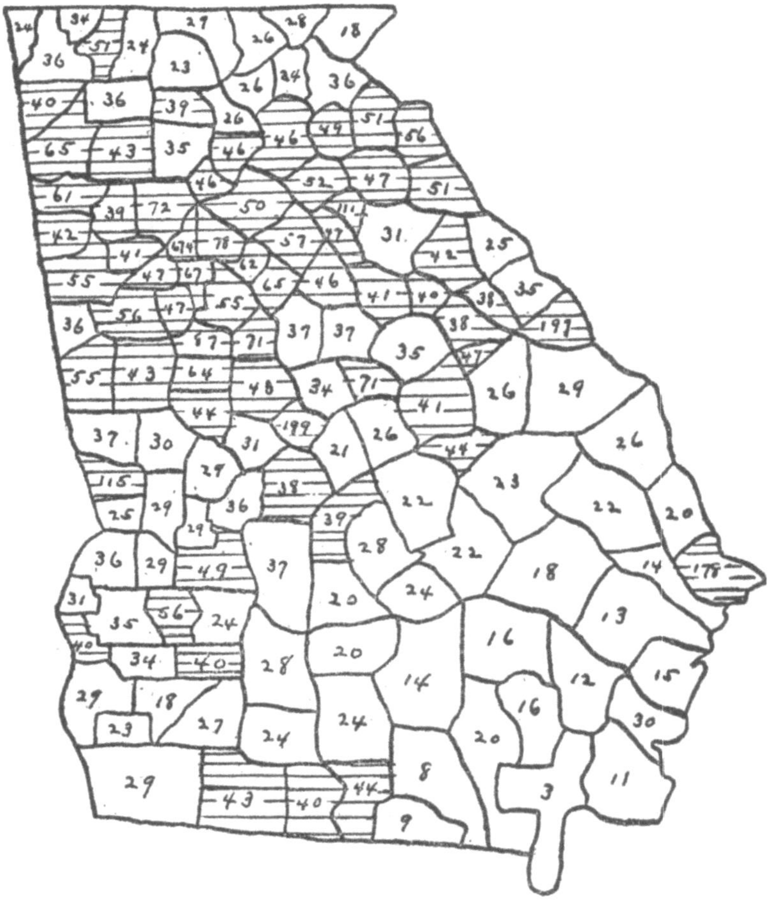

DENSITY OF POPULATION OF GEORGIA BY COUNTIES IN 1900. FOR THE STATE THERE ARE 37.6 PEOPLE PER SQUARE MILE. THE SHADED COUNTIES HAVE A GREATER DENSITY THAN THIS.

NEGROES FORM 46.7 PER CENT OF THE TOTAL POPULATION OF GEORGIA. IN THE SHADED COUNTIES THEY OUTNUMBER THE WHITES.

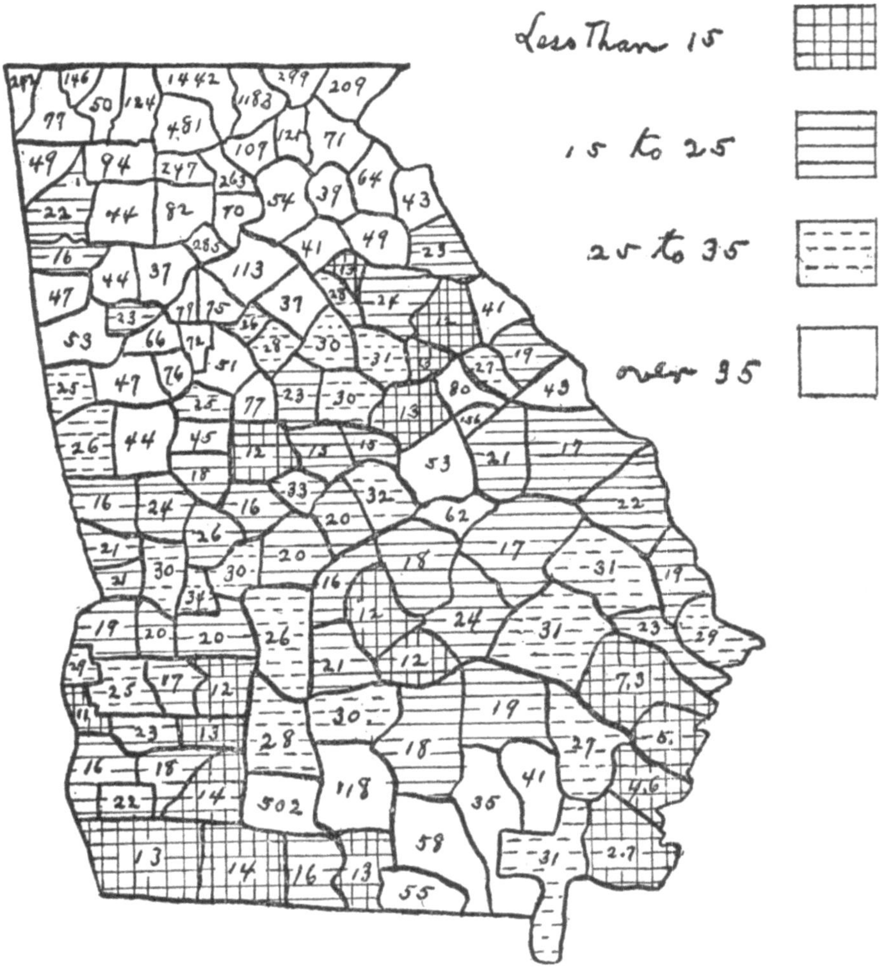

RATIO OF TOTAL IMPROVED ACREAGE TO NEGRO ACREAGE BY COUNTIES, 1903. RATIO FOR THE STATE IS 24.7, WHICH MEANS THAT NEGROES OWN ONE ACRE IN EVERY 24.7 ACRES. See Chapter IV of the text.

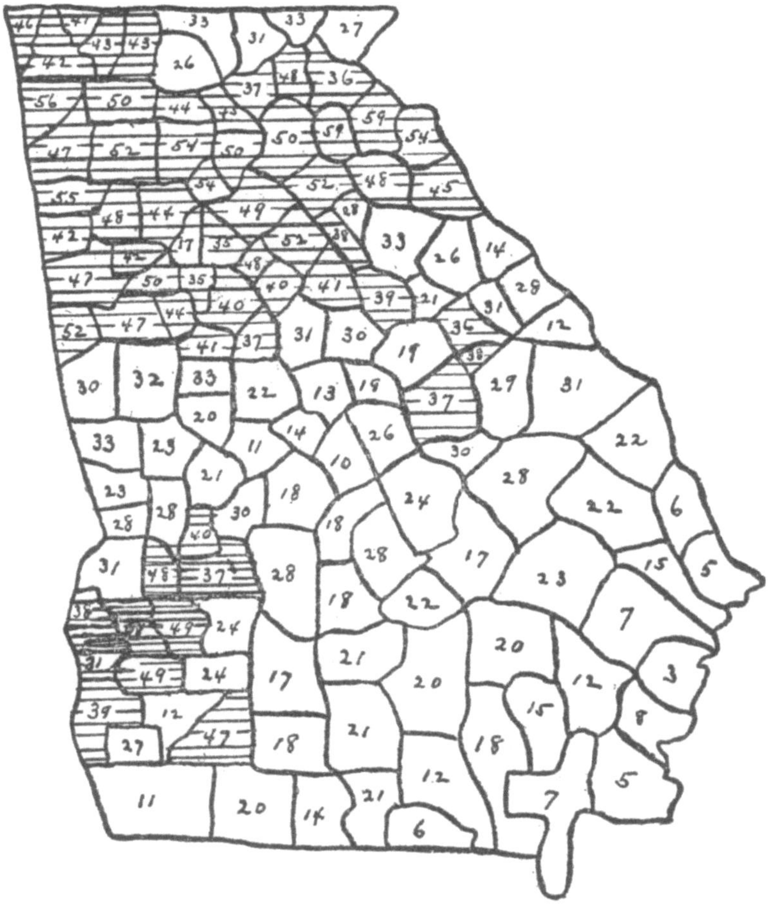

PERCENTAGE OF FARMS OPERATED BY SHARE TENANTS BY COUNTIES IN 1900. PERCENTAGE FOR THE STATE IS 34. COUNTIES OVER THIS ARE SHADED. See pp. 83–86 of the text.

PERCENTAGE OF FARMS OPERATED BY CASH TENANTS BY COUNTIES IN 1900. PERCENTAGE FOR THE STATE IS 26. COUNTIES OVER THIS ARE SHADED. See pp. 88–89 of the text.

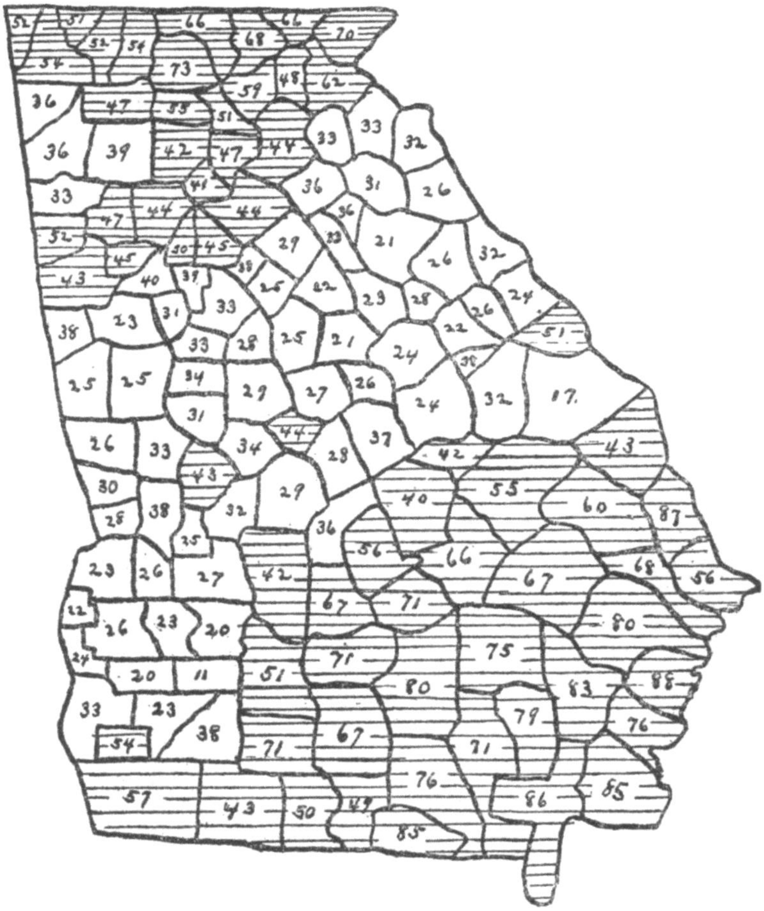

PERCENTAGE OF FARMS OPERATED BY OWNERS BY COUNTIES IN 1900. PERCENTAGE FOR THE STATE IS 40. COUNTIES OVER THIS ARE SHADED. See pp. 90–91 of the text.

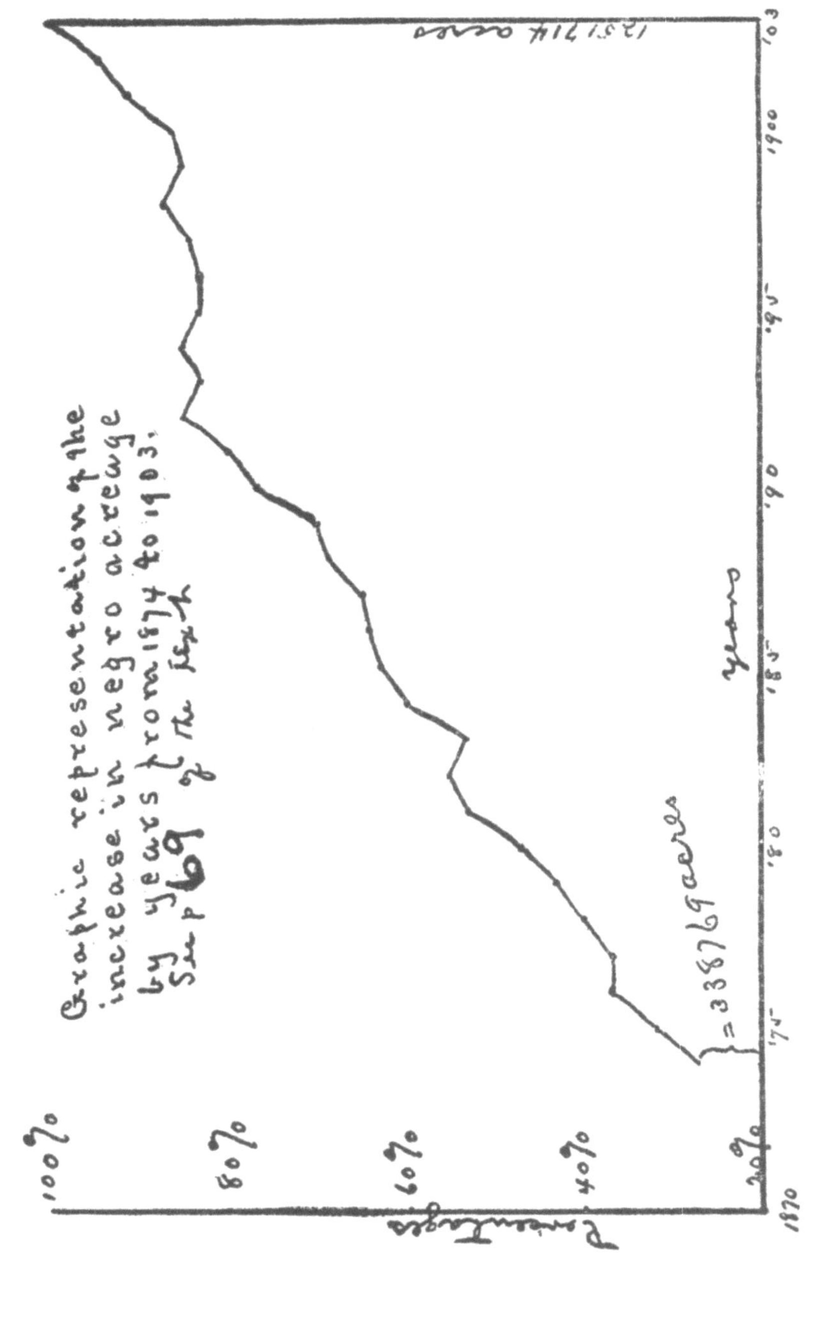
Graphic representation of the increase in negro acreage by years from 1874 to 1903. See p 69 of the text
Percentages
100%
80%
60%
40%
20%
1870
'75
'80
'85
'90
'95
1900
'03
years
= 338769 acres
1251714 acres

Bei Fragen zur Produktsicherheit wenden Sie sich bitte an:
If you have any questions regarding product safety,
please contact:

Walter de Gruyter GmbH
Genthiner Straße 13
10785 Berlin
productsafety@degruyterbrill.com